Supporting Someone Polyamorous

by the same the author

The Anxious Person's Guide to Non-Monogamy
Your Guide to Open Relationships, Polyamory and Letting Go
Lola Phoenix
Foreword by Kathy G. Slaughter
ISBN 978 1 83997 213 3
eISBN 978 1 83997 214 0

The Non-Monogamy Journal
90+ Scenarios and Questions to Define Boundaries
and Make Polyamory Work for You
Lola Phoenix
Foreword by Kathy G. Slaughter
ISBN 978 1 80501 422 5
eISBN 978 1 80501 423 2

of related interest

Monogamy? In this Economy??
Finances, Childrearing, and Other Practical Concerns of Polyamory
Laura Boyle
ISBN 978 1 80501 118 7
eISBN 978 1 80501 119 4

How to Understand Your Sexuality
A Practical Guide For Exploring Who You Are
Meg-John Barker and Alex Iantaffi
Illustrated by Jules Scheele
ISBN 978 1 78775 618 2
eISBN 978 1 78775 619 9

Queer Sex
A Trans and Non-Binary Guide to Intimacy, Pleasure and Relationships
Juno Roche
ISBN 978 1 78592 406 4
eISBN 978 1 78450 770 1

Supporting Someone Polyamorous

FAQs About Non-Monogamy and Allyship
for Family, Friends and Loved Ones

LOLA PHOENIX
FOREWORD BY RACHEL WRIGHT

Jessica Kingsley Publishers
London and Philadelphia

First published in Great Britain in 2025 by Jessica Kingsley Publishers
An imprint of John Murray Press

1

Copyright © Lola Phoenix 2025
Foreword copyright © Rachel Wright 2025

The right of Lola Phoenix to be identified as the Author of the Work has been
asserted by them in accordance with the Copyright, Designs and Patents Act 1988.

Front cover image source: Kara McHale. The cover image is for
illustrative purposes only, and any person featuring is a model.

A CIP catalogue record for this title is available from the
British Library and the Library of Congress

ISBN 978 1 80501 860 5
eISBN 978 1 80501 861 2

Printed and bound in the USA by Integrated Books International

Jessica Kingsley Publishers' policy is to use papers that are natural,
renewable and recyclable products and made from wood grown in
sustainable forests. The logging and manufacturing processes are expected
to conform to the environmental regulations of the country of origin.

Jessica Kingsley Publishers
Carmelite House
50 Victoria Embankment
London EC4Y 0DZ

www.jkp.com

John Murray Press
Part of Hodder & Stoughton Ltd
An Hachette Company

The authorised representative in the EEA is Hachette Ireland,
8 Castlecourt Centre, Dublin 15, D15 XTP3, Ireland (email: info@hbgi.ie)

Contents

Foreword

When I first came out as polyamorous, I felt so many different emotions: excitement, relief and fear. And while my friends and family were supportive, they didn't fully understand what polyamory meant or how to help me navigate its unique challenges. I found myself in conversations where, despite their good intentions, I didn't always know how to answer their questions – or they didn't know the right questions to ask. I wished for a resource to hand over and say, 'Here, read this. I love you, and this will help you understand and support me.' Thanks to Lola Phoenix and this book, that wish has come true – not just for me, but for anyone with a polyamorous loved one.

I've admired Lola's work for quite some time. While we both contribute to the conversation on polyamory and non-monogamy, we do so differently, and I've always really appreciated the unique content Lola has created, especially from her own lived experiences. She has shared her experiences with polyamory, including the anxiety she felt starting out and the lack of 'starter advice' available at the time. (Hello, similar experiences!) For those in non-monogamous relationships, explaining polyamory to loved ones can be daunting. Finding the right or best words to describe the experience can be challenging, and sharing with other people how they can be of support is hard when folks are often just figuring out what that even looks like for them. That's exactly where this book steps in, serving as a bridge to help loved ones understand not just the logistics of polyamory but also its emotions and nuances. For polyamorous folks like me, this book can ease some of the burden by offering a framework for those important conversations.

As a therapist, I work with many clients who are navigating non-monogamy. Some are in monogamous relationships, considering a transition to non-monogamy, while others are coming to terms with their polyamorous identity. One of the biggest challenges in the journey is explaining their choices or orientation to people they love. This book is an absolute go-to resource with an incredible format. I will recommend it to my clients, giving them something tangible to share with family and friends. Lola organizes the book into three main sections, which hit all the fundamentals needed for this conversation. Between understanding the terminology, addressing common concerns, learning how to provide genuine support, and so much more, it hits on the most important pieces of supporting someone polyamorous. Lola's writing is clear, thoughtful and practical, making a complex topic approachable and enjoyable.

Additionally, this book isn't just for those who have a polyamorous loved one – I think that polyamorous folks themselves will find value in the text. I genuinely think people will feel more comfortable sharing their polyamorous identity and experience after reading this book, having some sort of guide to help navigate these often emotional conversations. This guide could reduce the shame and anxiety that often surrounds coming out as polyamorous, helping folks feel more seen and supported – something vital for all of our mental health and well-being.

As more people live lives that reflect their genuine relationship orientations, resources like this will be essential in helping everyone feel at home in their relationships. As a therapist, I know how crucial it is to have accessible resources, especially outside of therapy, which can be expensive or difficult to access. Books like this make crucial information available to everyone, providing knowledge that can help reduce ignorance, judgement and anxiety. The antidote to these things is curiosity and understanding, which this book offers in abundance.

Rachel Wright, MA, LMFT, licensed psychotherapist
and host of The Wright Conversations Podcast

Introduction

I have been writing a relationship advice column and podcast for people in non-monogamous relationships since 2017 and have been polyamorous myself since 2010. I initially started writing about non-monogamy because I found most starter polyamory advice really unhelpful for me and felt alone in how much anxiety I was going through around non-monogamy.

In my writing, I wanted to help others starting out in polyamory understand that it's normal to feel anxious and unsure and that you don't have to feel like you're bad at polyamory just because you have emotions.

Throughout this time, I've also helped people navigate through the complexities of telling their family about being polyamorous. Because I am estranged from most of my family, I have experienced a lack of support in general, which was difficult. In some ways, having no support was simpler to deal with and I wrongly assumed that having family in your life would mean that you always had support.

It wasn't until I had a partner with a more complex relationship with their family that I got somewhat involved in that I realized the nuances involved and the toll it can personally take on an individual who wants to have a supportive family but also feels exhausted by the weight of explaining polyamory constantly. I went in search of some type of guide to provide a loved one and couldn't find anything recent so I decided to use my new experience and interview others about their experiences to build something that would make that experience a little easier.

At the time of writing this, I am not currently a parent and am undecided over whether that will change any time in my future. But, having been someone who desperately wanted to be a parent and as someone who has worked with 16–25-year-olds for over a decade, I can understand wanting the best for a young person or a child and being fearful for their future. In doing a lot of work within the LGBTQ community, especially within the trans community, I've come across many well-meaning but scared parents who don't know how to express the complexity of their desire for the best life for their child with the fear that they will not be accepted or embraced.

Though polyamory is not the same as being LGBTQ, I do believe that a lot of parents, family members and other people who want to support someone they love who is polyamorous likely face some of the same feelings. While the concept of marriage and what it means socially has shifted over the years from being a social contract to a celebration of love, most people have a socio-cultural understanding of monogamous pair bonding as 'natural' and the only type of bonding that is available.

'Open relationships' is a concept that has appeared more in the mainstream but not necessarily with any wide cultural acceptance or belief that these bonds are long-lasting or indeed 'healthy'. So for those people with limited understanding of what polyamory is, their exposure to the concept is limited to either this brief and shallow understanding or some of the more messy depictions of polyamory or something close to it available in the media.

With limited understanding, it isn't altogether surprising that people might be a little apprehensive for their loved one when they hear that they are interested in or involved with polyamory. It may be tempting as a polyamorous person with all of the context of the education, community and understanding they have gathered to feel betrayed or hurt when a family member questions them. The decision to live as one feels they always have been or to try polyamory as an active choice, and then to tell family members or loved ones about it is typically not done without a lot of consideration.

There is little I feel I can do if someone truly disrespects and rejects polyamory, though it's unlikely that includes anyone who is reading or has been given this book. If you're someone who truly wishes to support their loved one, I'm hoping this book can calm some of your fears and correct some misconceptions you may have. I can't promise you that your loved one will never have any bad experiences with polyamory (nor could I with monogamy either), but I can promise that if you provide genuine, loving support, that will help them cope with any issue they may face.

Part 1: Learning the Terms

Keep in mind as we go through these that this language is evolving as the needs evolve, so definitions may change as times and needs change.

1. WHAT IS POLYAMORY?

Polyamory is a way of organizing relationships where one is open to or has multiple romantic, sexual and/or important partner relationships in their lives. There are lots of ways to do polyamory, but the key difference between polyamory and 'open relationships' or 'non-monogamy' is that polyamory and polyamorous people focus on creating multiple deep relationships, whereas open relationships tend to involve one couple who have a deep relationship and who are free to develop other sexual relationships.

'Non-monogamy' is an umbrella term which can technically include *both* polyamory and open relationships. Obviously the distinction of what makes a relationship 'deep' is very individual and sometimes culturally influenced. But the critical difference is often that in polyamory, the end goal is to have multiple deep connections whereas many people who have an 'open relationship' may not be seeking that.

For someone who is supporting and loving a polyamorous person, the critical thing to understand about polyamory is that it is likely that there will be more than just one important person in your loved one's life and that you as a family member may play a critical role in the escalation, expansion or deepening of their relationship.

Monogamy typically involves an 'escalation' in the relationship. People meet, they date, they commit to exclusivity, they may get involved with each other's families, they move in with each other, they marry, they may have children and so on and so forth. While not everyone necessarily follows this pattern in monogamy, this is the narrative many people are used to.

Within polyamory, many may still follow this style of escalation with one or more partners – or some may choose not to do some of these things with any of their partners. For some people, they can have deep relationships with others without ever living together. For others, they may have just one partner they seek to involve their family with – and some choose this out of fear of involving their families. They may tell their families or loved ones about polyamory or they may not.

As someone seeking to support a loved one, the best thing you can do is ask your loved one what part you can play in making them feel supported in their identity. Depending on your relationship with them, they may not come to you specifically for relationship advice (especially if they wouldn't for monogamy), but if you allow yourself to be someone they can introduce their partners to, you could represent part of the development of their relationships.

2. WORDS YOU MIGHT RUN INTO

I hope you like learning new words – because there are a fair few words to learn. Since you're supporting someone who is polyamorous rather than practising it yourself, you don't have quite as much to learn, but here are some basic definitions that might make your conversations with your loved one and anything else you read a little more clear:

metamour: People who also date your partner but who you do not date. For example, in the diagram below, Partner A and B are metamours. They do not date each other. Partners B and C date each other so they are not metamours, but partners.

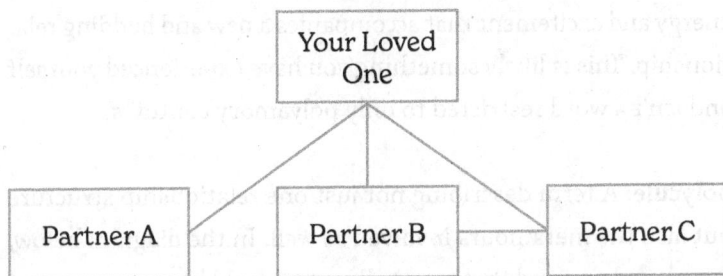

```
                    ┌──────────────┐
                    │  Your Loved  │
                    │     One      │
                    └──────────────┘
                   ╱       │        ╲
      ┌───────────┐  ┌───────────┐  ┌───────────┐
      │ Partner A │  │ Partner B │──│ Partner C │
      └───────────┘  └───────────┘  └───────────┘
```

compersion: Sometimes described as 'the opposite of jealousy', compersion is a feeling of joy or happiness in witnessing or hearing about a partner's attraction or love for another person and/or relationship successes or wins. Example: When Martha told me about how well her date went, I felt so much compersion! This word can sometimes be used outside of partnerships, though some people would only refer to compersion within a relationship context.

hinge: This is a person who is between two partners. For example in the diagram below, your loved one would be the 'hinge' between Partner A and Partner B. This particular structure is also called a 'V' relationship.

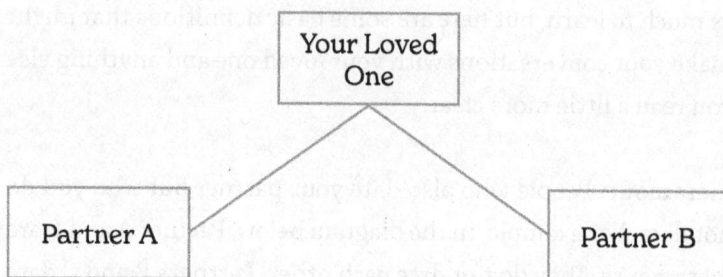

```
                    ┌─────────────┐
                    │ Your Loved  │
                    │    One      │
                    └─────────────┘
                       /       \
      ┌───────────┐   /         \   ┌───────────┐
      │ Partner A │                 │ Partner B │
      └───────────┘                 └───────────┘
```

new relationship energy (NRE): A term describing the rush of energy and excitement that accompanies a new and budding relationship. This is likely something you have experienced yourself and isn't a word restricted to only polyamory contexts.

polycule: A term describing not just one relationship structure but also the metamours involved as well. In the diagram below, your loved one and Partners A, B and C would be seen as part of the same 'polycule'.

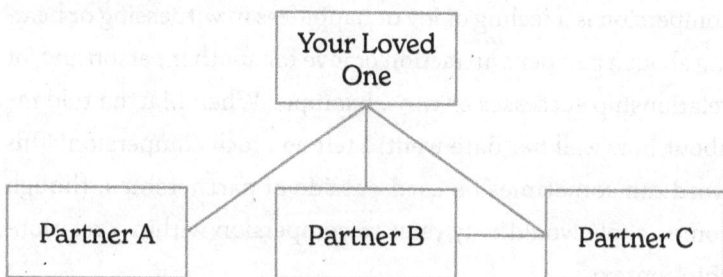

```
                    ┌─────────────┐
                    │ Your Loved  │
                    │    One      │
                    └─────────────┘
                    /      |      \
   ┌───────────┐  /   ┌───────────┐   ┌───────────┐
   │ Partner A │      │ Partner B │───│ Partner C │
   └───────────┘      └───────────┘   └───────────┘
```

3. POLYAMORY VERSUS POLYGAMY

Folks who might not have been aware that Facebook had an 'Open relationships' option for relationship status may only know about polyamory through the subject of polygamy. *Technically* polygamy involves a practice of marrying multiple spouses, and is not restricted to only men having multiple wives. Polyamory doesn't technically have to involve marriage. In many places, polygamy is outlawed through the criminalization of either adultery, or bigamy, which means marrying multiple spouses.

However, when most people picture or think of polygamy, they are thinking of polygyny, which is where a man has multiple wives but a woman cannot have multiple husbands. I think it's fair to say that most people don't have a positive opinion about polygamy, and the perception of polygamy is that it's often associated with exploitation of women and cult-like behaviours. Without an understanding of polyamory and what it is, if you believed that polyamory was like polygamy, it's understandable that you could have an instant fear of your child being involved in a cult or being exploited.

You can breathe though. Polygamy is not the same as polyamory. While I can't really comment about the way polygamy is practised in some religious contexts and in other countries, I can safely say the main differences between polygamy and how it's historically practised versus polyamory is that polyamory is not gender restrictive. Polygamy typically only allows for one man to have multiple wives whereas polyamory allows for people of any gender to have however many partners they wish and have the time for.

While polygamy is typically culturally encouraged within some societies, to the best of my knowledge, no community is currently culturally encouraging polyamory – though some people may feel that in their subcultures, polyamory is definitely more common or more usual than monogamy. While there may be some cases where people try polyamory to avoid a breakup, most people are not forced into practising polyamory and don't even know polyamory is really an option until much later in life.

One could class polygamy as a form of non-monogamy, but the two communities are not really very similar or even in contact with each other, as far as I can tell. In my nearly 15 years now of being involved in non-monogamous communities, I've yet to come across a person who describes themselves as polygamous in the way people envision it within those communities. So it is safe to say, especially if a loved one has given you this book, it is unlikely they are participating in the polygamy that you might be thinking of.

4. DIFFERENT RELATIONSHIP STYLES

There are lots of different ways to do monogamy, even if you come from a culture which has one picture of the typical relationship. Some people live together, some don't. Some people have long-distance relationships. Some have children, some don't. Two people being monogamous doesn't necessarily guarantee that they will be compatible in terms of their lifestyles and how they want to live their lives.

The same can be said of polyamory. There are lots of different ways to do polyamory and it is sometimes helpful, if you want to support someone who is polyamorous, to understand the different ways they might be practising it.

Before we jump into the complicated aspects of the different ways that people have relationships, it's important to help you understand what makes a 'relationship' and how those things 'progress'.

A Note on Relationship 'Progression'

Monogamy makes defining what a 'relationship' is fairly easy for most – the exclusivity of romantic and sexual feelings with one person is part and parcel of what defines them as a 'partner'. But when you have friendships that can include 'benefits' or when you are allowed to explore other options and let relationships develop, where does that come in? Ultimately, this is something that is down to your loved one. If you're a family member, you may not be particularly interested in knowing the ins and outs of your loved one's sex life – that's okay. But understanding that they may not define a 'partner' in a way that you expect is one way you can be supportive.

Another aspect of polyamory that requires some rethinking is the concept of 'progression' within relationships. We have what I call a cultural script of monogamy within many societies – you meet, you date, you move in together, you marry, you have children, etc. Not everyone follows this script even within monogamy and this script has certainly changed, and varies depending on the time, location and surrounding culture. However, we have a shared cultural understanding that a deeper commitment through these cultural milestones creates a 'safer' or more 'established' relationship.

Your loved one may be interested in hitting these milestones with one or more partners, or they may not be interested in any of these milestones with anyone. Because many cultures define

21

the 'specialness' of a romantic relationship around exclusivity and meeting these milestones with just one person, it may be difficult to comprehend how these milestones can be meaningful if they aren't exclusive to one person, and that's okay. We will expand more on the topic of exclusivity later, but at this stage it may be worth mentioning that some of the relationship milestones that are common in monogamous-centric (or mono-centric) culture may not be exclusive to one person in your polyamorous loved one's life.

Some polyamorous people may not even wish to meet *any* of these milestones. There are other ways that people choose to measure the depth or establishment of their relationship that aren't these specific milestones. It's understandable if you have a moment of sadness if you had set yourself the expectation of doing something as typical as walking your loved one down the aisle during a wedding. It's okay to have that sadness, but understand that your loved one can have a rich, enjoyable and committed relationship with someone without needing to hit these milestones.

It's important to differentiate between an expectation your culture has given you about the life your child might lead, what story that tells you about their happiness or capacity for fulfilment, and what they are actually experiencing and telling you. In some societies and in previous times, it might have been culturally typical for a father, for example, to express disappointment that he will never play football with his child if he has a girl. But we have grown as a society to understand that being a girl is not a limiting factor on that experience and our culture now may tell that dad a very different story.

Over time, our culture may give us a different narrative about marriage and long-term partnership, especially in an age where so many people are defining themselves as failures if their marriage doesn't work out the way they wanted it to – even though they are not failures at all. Until then, hopefully this can make you aware that some of those fears you may have about your loved one being polyamorous are coming from a culture that has told you a story about happiness and how to attain it – and that that story is a story that only fits some people and doesn't fit many others. And that's okay!

Now, let's go through some of the basic terms and set-ups here and address some concerns you may have with these as well as ways that you can engage your loved one in conversations to learn more about what they're interested in.

Hierarchical Polyamory

This is one of the most common types of polyamory because quite a few people do not even hear about polyamory as an option until they are already in a monogamous relationship. Within this set-up, a person who is polyamorous usually has one primary partner, whom they often live with, and with that partner they often seek some of those milestones we mentioned before that involve deeper and/or legal commitments. They may desire to only have those with one partner and have other relationships outside of this, but spend the lion's share of their time with the partner they live with, who may be called their primary, anchor or nesting partner.

It's important to note that relationships that someone has outside of their primary (sometimes called 'secondary partners') are not necessarily less important or less emotionally valuable than the relationship they have with a primary. It can be easy to see a hierarchy as a reflection of love, because we're often encouraged in mono-centric culture to see our romantic partner as at the top of our overall relationship hierarchy and to always prioritize them, but that is not actually the case for every single person or their experience.

Where you come in as someone who wants to support a polyamorous loved one is that meeting any of their partners may be part of their process of deepening their relationship with that person. Just as meeting parents is a milestone within monogamous relationships, it can also be part of that process for many polyamorous people. Your loved one may also wish to bring multiple partners to a family event, and being open and willing to work with that may be something that you can do as someone who wants to be supportive. If your loved one practises hierarchical polyamory, asking them enthusiastically about where meeting you comes into their relationship development may be a welcome discussion.

Solo Polyamory

Typically, solo polyamorists are people who do not desire to hit any of the cultural milestones typical of monogamous relationships with any partner. Quite often they enjoy living on their own or with roommates and choose intentionally to not live with partners, not to marry, and sometimes not meet family. Individual boundaries will vary, but it's fair to say that most solo polyamorous people will have a different way of defining how their relationships with others deepen and/or become more committed without a typical social narrative.

The important aspect to understand about this is that solo

polyamory is a conscious decision, not indecision. It's not a reflection of a lack of ability or desire to commit to anyone. On the contrary, many solo polyamorous people are deeply committed to the people in their life. Choosing not to live with a partner is not a sign of a lack of love or a lack of commitment. It can be easy to see relationships like that as less foundational or less solid because of our cultural influences, but what defines the depth of a relationship will depend on the person.

Where you can be supportive of your loved one, if they are solo polyamorous, is asking where you come into their relationship progression. They may not want to bring any partners 'home' per se or they may see coming home as part of the way they progress with relationships. It may be even more important for solo polyamorous people to be able to bring more than one partner to an event. Enthusiastically asking your loved one how you can be supportive as well as respecting the way they choose to do their relationships and not assuming that they are not 'serious' is a great way to show your support.

Relationship Anarchy

This is more of an overall philosophy of how to do all relationships than just a relationship style. Relationship anarchy is a term coined by Andie Nordgren in the 2006 essay 'The short instructional manifesto for relationship anarchy'. It is a way of applying anarchist principles to relationships focusing on anti-hierarchy, respect of individual autonomy and compassion. It's okay if that definition doesn't make it clear for you – if you're unfamiliar with anarchist principles, you may even be slightly alarmed.

What this means in practice is that your loved one desires to see all of their relationships – romantic, friends, family, etc. – as equal. They reject the idea that one relationship should be held over another or prioritized over another. As such, they're unlikely to engage in some of the relationship milestones we mentioned before or may refuse to restrict them to one person. They may have friendships in their life or platonic romantic relationships that they value as much as romantic sexual relationships. The difference between this and solo polyamory is that a solo poly-amorous person may still prioritize romantic relationships over other types, whereas a relationship anarchist believes in breaking all of that down.

Where you can be supportive of your loved one is by asking them what role you play within their overall relationship dynamic. Be open to them inviting a variety of different types of people as their 'plus one' (and be willing to expand it to a plus two or more in some cases) and that their relationship with that person may not look the way you would expect. In this case you can assume that all of their relationships hold an equal value to them, including your relationship with them. Ask questions, be open and curious and also rethink your assumptions about what makes a relationship deep or serious.

Kitchen Table and Garden Party Polyamory

Many people have noted that the old 'traditional' (though not actually traditional) model of the family of a husband who works and a stay-at-home wife is not even possible in the current economy. There is a running joke within many polyamory communities about how polyamory helps people save on rental expenses and shared streaming accounts. That's probably not the actual reason your loved one might choose to practise kitchen table or garden party polyamory, but living with multiple partners definitely has economical and time benefits.

Kitchen table polyamory is generally where someone desires a lifestyle where all of their partners get along and perhaps even all live together within a co-op type of format. The goal is to form a family that would gather, happily, around a kitchen table every night. Garden party polyamory is similar to this but is a little less formal and instead seeks a situation where partners might mix and mingle as they would at a garden party and have friendly relationships, but not necessarily be akin to family. Both styles are desiring something that isn't quite solo polyamory but isn't necessarily hierarchical either.

Where you can be supportive as a loved one here is, again, to ask about whether or not you meeting their partners could be part of deepening their relationships. For people in kitchen table-style relationships especially, the ability to bring more than one partner to an event may be very important, so being respectful of that is also important. Respecting all of their partners as an equal part of their life and not using old narratives to assume one is more 'important' can be crucial. People can also practise kitchen table polyamory with partners they live with and still have other partnerships outside of that dynamic.

Parallel Polyamory

Almost the opposite of kitchen table polyamory, parallel polyamory involves a situation where you have other relationships but those partners never interact, or there is no inherent desire for partners to interact with one another. This doesn't mean that relationships are hidden from each other or that people have a problem with meeting other partners, but that there is no expectation of meeting other partners, and in some cases, the person dating multiple people may feel better when they don't 'cross the streams'.

I think a lot of monogamous people might relate to this when thinking about the different types of friendships they have. Some friends you have could be cool with one another and everyone could hang out in a big group and have a good time. Whereas you may have some friends who actively wouldn't get along or who just wouldn't mix well together because you enjoy different things with different people. The same could be said of parallel polyamory.

As a loved one, where you can be supportive is, again, asking openly where your involvement can be beneficial. Parallel polyamory is sometimes coupled with a hierarchical structure, but not always. Some solo polyamorous people prefer to operate in a parallel way and some people who are relationship anarchists will still be very parallel in how they approach their relationships. How you fit into this might be different but it is less likely a loved one practising parallel polyamory will be interested in bringing more than one partner to any event.

Don't Ask, Don't Tell (DADT)

Most individuals who practise DADT don't typically call themselves polyamorous. For that reason, it's unlikely they would pick up this book or seek support from family members, because a critical aspect of DADT is not telling anyone, including family. Many people in polyamorous communities are against policies

28

like DADT because it involves secrecy. However, I feel it's worth mentioning just in case so that you have a broader awareness of non-monogamy. Don't ask, don't tell is a practice wherein a couple allows for one member of the couple (usually a married heterosexual couple), though sometimes both, to seek experiences outside of their relationship. Usually, it is understood that these will not be full-on romantic relationships and the partner with the ticket to explore is usually allowed one night or specific time frames where they can explore. The rule, as the name suggests, is that the partner with the ticket to explore makes every effort to not mention and hide the presence of their outside activities.

As I mentioned, this practice is heavily criticized and considered unethical within polyamory communities for understandable reasons. I mention it because I believe as a family member, if your loved one is engaging in this practice in any capacity, what they will undoubtedly need regardless of what happens with this set-up, is a kind, non-judgemental presence in their life. Regardless of anyone's individual opinion of ethics, I personally think that if this is something that has been agreed to by two adults, then how they wish to define their relationships is up to them.

You likely have your own opinions about the ethics or longevity of this type of set-up and those are yours to have. I would urge you as a loved one to consider whether or not expressing those opinions in this context would really get you where you ultimately want to go. If we look at this scenario as a loved one and envision the potential outcomes, should this end badly, what you want is for your loved one to be able to overcome this situation and move on to find a better situation in the future. Having someone in their life who has remained non-judgemental of them and always provided support is a soft landing place when coming out of any type of difficult or tough relationship.

If it does not end badly and works functionally for all parties involved, your loved one may still struggle with everyone else's judgements or assumptions. You could become one of their very few sources of support, and would that be something you would want to take away? I can understand being concerned for your loved one, but sometimes (excluding situations where people are in immediate physical danger), being able to hold back your personal opinion to provide someone you love with the support they need is a pathway towards their overall improvement and self-esteem.

Triads, Quads and More

As I previously mentioned, a good deal of people don't discover that non-monogamy is an option until they are already within a pre-existing monogamous relationship. As a result, the first thing that many people think of as a 'safe' option to protect their existing partnership is an 'opening up' to include a 'third'. I feel like it is unlikely that your loved one is one of those people or perhaps tried to do this initially and did not have a good experience or thought better of it. While there are many reasons I don't encourage people to try to find a 'third' that I won't go into here, there are many situations where organically people end up in what is called a 'triad' or a 'thruple', or four people who end up as a 'quad'.

It's important to know that even within the polyamory community, people have their reservations about these types of relationships and their 'difficulty'. A lot of people who desire to be in a triad or who are trying out a triad for the first time may struggle to find people even within their community who are supportive. While this can really depend on the whole context of the situation, I think the most important thing to understand as a person wanting to support your loved one is that you can provide them with a solid source of non-judgemental support.

Providing an environment where you welcome their two or three partners openly and as you would with a monogamous loved one is important. It is likely that the equity they have between partners is important to them and therefore if meeting you is part of their deepening of relationships, it may be important that meeting you is not something that only one part of the triad or quad does.

It may also be important to understand that, even while your loved one may live with or be within a triad, they may also have partners outside of this formation who have equal importance to them. Having a triad or a quad doesn't necessarily mean those relationships are prioritized over other romantic relationships. Understanding the role that you play within the relationship progression, if they have any, is really important and asking your loved one how you can be supportive of their relationship dynamic here as well is also helpful.

Polyfidelity

Polyfidelity is generally uncommon within polyamory circles, but I thought it was worth mentioning just in case. Polyfidelity often occurs within people who are in triads or quads where they agree within the group that they will not bring in new partners or date others outside of that formation. Generally speaking, because people desire the freedom that polyamory can bring them in terms of having new relationships, they will not be all that interested in an agreement that in effect does not allow them to have any new relationships.

People commit to a polyfidelitous relationship for all sorts of reasons, and if it's something that your loved one has committed to, then you can take similar steps to the ones I've advised in the section 'Triads, Quads and More' above to show your support. If your loved one is polyfidelitous, they may invest in the traditional relationship milestones but do so with more than one partner. Support that you can provide in the process of deepening those relationships equally will be helpful.

Open Relationships

This is a wide umbrella term that a lot of people use interchangeably with 'polyamory', 'ethical non-monogamy' and 'non-monogamy' but technically, many people would define an open relationship as one where a couple is 'open' but only to other sexual relationships. Relationships that are opened up purely for the chance for partners to have sexual explorations outside of their main partnership don't tend to be ones that people disclose to their family members or loved ones – not necessarily due to shame or judgement but mostly because of the understandable boundary people have in discussing their sex lives with people they are related to.

However, there may be reasons your loved one may choose to disclose this to you. You're definitely within your rights to have boundaries around what you discuss but if your loved one chooses to discuss this with you, it's more likely that they need some support or a listening ear that they may struggle to find outside of their peer support group. You can provide support by being there for them if they need someone to talk to, depending on your comfort level.

For All Relationship Types

This is a growing and changing community and lifestyle. It's important to remember that monogamous marriage and partnership is not the same in our society now as it has been in centuries past. Marriage was once the exchange of property (consider the word 'animal husbandry') and romantic love was once seen as a type of madness. The concept of having an official 'partner' while being free to explore other sexual opportunities is also not necessarily new and has previously been available to a select few people with social power.

But 'polyamory' as we know it today is a relatively new word, concept and approach to love and relationships and as such definitions change and new words are emerging all of the time. You may see this as a bit scary – which is understandable. There is a certain humanity in wanting stability, control and being afraid of change. However, just because something is new does not mean it is unstable, and just because something is older does not mean it is 'safe'. Even as I publish this book, there may be new relationship styles that grow and form that your loved one may fall under.

For most of these styles, you've likely noticed some pretty common themes that pop up for you as a loved one in terms of the support you offer. Providing your loved one with a safe, non-judgemental space to land is something that all relationship types (even monogamy) can benefit from. Reserving your own opinion about how you define relationships, what 'success' means and understanding where the narrative around relationships and what they culturally mean is also something that will benefit your loved one.

Another common theme is your loved one's ability to bring more than one partner to an event and the treatment you give to partners. The easiest way for you to understand the importance of treating partners equitably is to imagine how you might be if your loved one brought different friends home. You probably wouldn't treat one friend any different to the other. There may be ways in which you mesh or gel well with some of your loved ones' friends and not others, but there should be no inherent desire to see one friendship as 'more important' than another. Approach your loved one's partners with a similar lens if that is something that they have requested from you.

Let's get to the elephant in the room though – having more than one partner attend an event might be a little awkward for you and/or other family members. That's okay! As much as your loved one is operating without a cultural script, so are you. There are, to the date of writing, no common cultural representations of any type of polyamory that are represented as healthy and stable, let alone a triad or a quad, and no representations of loved ones bringing home more than one partner, so it is understandable that this might feel awkward. Talk about it with one another. Sometimes I find dealing with the awkwardness of newness is easiest to do if you're just honest about it and embrace it.

I also want to reiterate that it's okay for you to experience worry and fear for your loved one. As I mentioned before, you have likely been given a narrative about your culture and what a 'good life' is for your loved one, and them going off of the script is a little bit scary! What's important is learning how to work through these fears with a therapist or with another non-judgemental third party who might be able to listen and understand your fears.

Expressing those fears to your loved one, especially if you are in a position of power as an older relative or parent, may do the opposite of what you want. They may feel judged or pushed away by your fear. They may feel even more pressure to stay within a dysfunctional polyamorous relationship in order to 'prove' the relationship style is valid. They may be less likely to come to you for help should something go wrong in any type of relationship they have. What you want to provide them with is a space where they can truly be themselves and be accepted for it. You're welcome to have your own fears, feelings and misconceptions, but it's important to practise some discernment about when you express those.

Lastly, the biggest advice I would give about you supporting a polyamorous loved one in their relationship type is that how people practise polyamory can be unique to them and so understanding them as an individual rather than just a relationship type is important. Talk about these things with your loved one. Try to avoid assuming what will be important to them or what anything means. Challenge your own perceptions about the depth of relationships and how one measures them.

I firmly believe that even people who are monogamous can benefit from unpacking some of the things monogamous-centric cultures have taught them throughout the years. It is fully possible that you might find that there are ways that *you* don't fit within the current cultural script of monogamy – and that's okay. I'm not saying you will become polyamorous or that you have to, but I do genuinely think that the process of learning about other options can make people feel more confident and empowered in the choices that they make.

5. WHEN TO BE CONCERNED

As I've said before, fear and concern about your loved one practising polyamory is to be expected. You're operating outside of a cultural script and sometimes challenging the narratives you thought spelled success for your loved one. You're definitely allowed to have those feelings and I want to encourage you to explore those feelings with a therapist and to practise some discernment when deciding to discuss these things with your loved one directly.

But as someone who is wanting to support a loved one, I think it is also prudent for you to understand when there are reasons to be concerned. Just like any relationship you have likely had in your life, it is sometimes difficult to figure out if you're incompatible with the person or if that person is actually a jerk! This is something I think we struggle with in all facets of your life.

While I still maintain that the best thing you can do as a loved one is to provide a non-judgemental space for your loved one to return to, it may be helpful for you to understand some of the more unethical practices that people stumble upon so that you can be prepared to offer support. Some of these situations you may not be fully aware of until they have already happened and are over, but having an understanding of the basic meanings and problems with them may allow you to provide support directly and avoid the question and answer session when your loved one is in expressing or experiencing intense emotions or distress.

OPP/Harem Building

No, not the Naughty by Nature song and yes, I am that old. This is a practice referred to in polyamory communities as a 'one penis policy' (OPP), which generally means that, within a man and woman couple, the woman in the couple is only allowed to date other women. There are a lot of issues people within the polyamory community have with OPPs. It ignores the existence of transgender people, it generally isn't applied fairly (as the man is not expected to only date other men), and many people feel this policy reflects the belief that sapphic relationships are less threatening or serious than heterosexual relationships. Specifically when a man is looking for multiple women who will only date him or only date him and the other women within their group, this is referred to as harem building.

In general, while there are definitely men who see women as less of a 'threat' to their relationship, it has been my experience that I have way less anxiety and fear when my partner is dating or sleeping with someone with whom I am less able to compare my body or gender. I believe some inexperienced people create this policy out of fear and as a result of comparing themselves to others rather than a belief that sapphic relationships are not a 'threat'. However, as understandable as this fear may be, generally speaking this policy is misguided and unfair.

There are cases where women who have a man for a partner will decide themselves that they are purely interested in dating other women, but this would not usually be described as an OPP. If your loved one is engaged in an OPP or has had a partner request this, it may not be something that they disclose immediately to you, depending on your relational boundaries. If they do disclose this to you, it may not be something about which they want advice from you.

In that case, I think the support you can offer is, rather than outwardly telling them to leave the relationship, asking them what they want out of a relationship. If your loved one is the person pushing for this policy, you could ask them if this policy would really prevent their partner from leaving them or replacing them. But I want to stress, these are light questions, not meant to pass judgement on what your loved one is doing but to get them to think deeply – but only if they are open to it. Trying to push them into an intellectual exploration of the issue if they are not interested in exploring it may just push them away from you in general.

There are some people who are fine with this restriction from their partner, even if it is technically unfair, and I hesitate to try and control their relationship. It is likely, if they have tried to enter into a polyamorous community, that they have already experienced some pushback from the community about this policy. Chances are, whether you were given this book or found it yourself, you want to be that place of comfort for your loved one. Be there to provide them the support they need.

Unicorn Hunting

When a lot of people open their relationship for the first time, they are reasonably and understandably worried about losing the relationship they already have. Some people decide to respond to this fear by looking together for a third partner, as mentioned previously in the section '4. Different Relationship Styles' above. For a lot of people new to polyamory, they think this is a lot 'safer'.

People looking on their own for new polyamorous relationships may find a couple 'looking for a third'. In some cases, there are couples who opt for trying to find a 'third' because they are worried about dating individually and then there are others who present the woman in the couple as a single queer woman on dating sites to find women and then springing the news that they are a couple during the first few dates. The spectrum of these behaviours are called unicorn hunting.

This is a heavily criticized and disliked practice within the polyamory community – whether it is done by a well-meaning couple or someone intentionally trying to deceive others. The probability that the couple will dump the third person to 'save' their relationship is extremely high and quite a lot of people have been burned in polyamory by being sacrificed at the altar of coupledom. The couple may not have intended to do this and may have genuinely wanted to find another person they could see as an equal within a triad, but the reality is that there is often a power imbalance they are not acknowledging.

Not all triads are unicorn hunting and there may be some cases where a person dates both of the people in the couple and it evolves into a triad relationship without 'the couple' going out together to find someone. I have heard of single bisexual women who have had positive experiences with many couples and prefer to date couples. Your mileage here may vary depending on what's involved. But as a supportive loved one, again, providing a non-judgemental space is crucial.

Generally speaking, the couples who intend well typically recalibrate their approach when they learn why unicorn hunting isn't very ethical or even an ideal way to date. The ones who insist on dating as a couple are unlikely, I feel, to listen to a loved one tell them anything about the ethical problems in their relationships. Likewise, I tend to find that people who want to go forward with dating a couple don't tend to want to change their course when confronted with information about ethics either.

The people who tend to be open to reconsidering their approach tend to have things that come up that they don't like about their relationships and don't know if they should listen to themselves about these early warning signs. Where you can be supportive is by providing a listening ear and asking your loved one what they want out of the relationships they have. Staying open to the concept of polyamory in general, even if you're not wanting your loved one to be mistreated, is key. You may have to spend some time establishing trust with your loved one first before having conversations with them about issues within their relationship because it's likely they have already been told that polyamory is the problem, not the relationship style or approach.

Veto

This is another type of behaviour that I believe people lean on out of fear or desperation. It is where one partner has the right to 'veto' or demand a partner break up with someone. This can be something that is granted when the relationship starts or something that ends up happening through an ultimatum when someone is upset. This is generally seen as a controlling, manipulative move by the polyamory community and is incredibly discouraged.

Throughout my years of giving advice, rarely have I seen situations where people have given their partner veto power from the start. Most of the time, it seems like people end up giving their partner an ultimatum because they are desperate. Either they are experiencing a lot of emotional turmoil or they have a partner who is super focused on their new relationship and they are feeling ignored. This doesn't mean it's okay to try and control your partner's relationships, but I think it's important to look at this with compassion.

There are all sorts of ways you might provide support for your loved one. In any situation – whether they are the one issuing a veto, receiving a veto request or getting vetoed – they will likely have strong emotions about the situation and need support and care. If you are reading this book, it is likely your loved one is not trying to control anybody or hurt anybody so if they are involved in a veto, it's a difficult situation where they might need someone to just listen and give them a space to talk.

Isolation

This is something of a concern even within monogamy but it's generally not a good sign when someone convinces your loved one to cease contact with their friends or loved ones. There is a lot more here I can write about the dynamics of abusive relationships, what signs to look out for, and how to support someone in an abusive relationship but I would advise actually checking out *Why Does He Do That?* by Lundy Bancroft, which gives a much better background of how to properly support someone than I can.

But primarily, if your relationship with your loved one changes, they reach out less or they have cut you off completely with no explanation, this might be cause for checking out Bancroft's book or reaching out to local resources for people in abusive relationships, such as relationship charities and hotlines.

Making Mistakes

It's easy when you're approaching a relationship style that's new to forget the way we all stumbled into relationships in our earlier years. Sometimes I feel like people put an expectation on themselves in polyamory to know everything because they tend to read a lot more about polyamory than they ever did about dating or monogamy when they were younger.

But making mistakes is part of life and when feelings are involved, it's much easier for us to make mistakes that we normally wouldn't make otherwise. Sometimes as loved ones we want to do our best to protect our loved one from ever feeling any pain, and that is understandable. But sometimes trying to protect our loved ones results in them feeling more distant from us or stifles their growth. Give your loved one the space to make their own mistakes where possible even if it involves an OPP, veto or other practices frowned upon. You can be concerned, but make sure you stay part of your life.

∞

Part 2: Frequently Voiced Concerns

INTRODUCTION

Now that you've had a little bit of an introduction to polyamory, the most common types of relationship styles, and some of the issues you may run across, I will address some of the concerns that a polyamorous person's loved ones may have. In many situations, loved ones have concerns that they can't directly discuss with the polyamorous person.

I compare this to situations I have seen and gone through in the LGBTQ community with significant others, friends and family members. When family members come out, their loved ones have a lot of questions, and there are specific groups for loved ones so that these questions can be answered without the burden it can sometimes place on the people already coping with coming out or dealing with an unwelcoming society.

While the obstacles faced by polyamorous people are different to those faced by the LGBTQ community, answering these questions can sometimes be difficult emotionally for polyamorous people, and my goal with answering some of these here both from the experience I have had in providing advice for others as well as my own experience, is to help loved ones both to understand a little bit more and also to be able to feel a bit more settled.

Not every single one of these questions will be applicable or relevant for all loved ones, so, if you decide to read through them individually, you may encounter a repetition of some concepts.

1. IS THIS A PHASE?

This question can apply to so many identities, but given the way polyamory is not reflected in modern culture and media, it's understandable that you might be worried about the longevity of polyamory. While for your loved one it may feel like this is a sign you don't take polyamory as a serious path, I feel like your concern comes from a place of wanting your loved one to have stability within their life and to not have to experience pain.

Polyamory Regret

I can't tell you whether or not your loved one will be in polyamorous relationships for the rest of their lives. Polyamory may be part of what they feel is their core identity or it may be something that they try for a few years and then change their mind about. The unfortunate side effect of polyamory as a choice being a somewhat new way to describe a practice that isn't that new is that there is often little in the way of research on the community.

Not to mention, there is a small sample size in general of polyamorous people that, even if one were to weather a group, the statistical significance of different aspects of that group may be difficult to parse. Data is often much more able to address concerns when there is a lot more of it available and there is only now just beginning to be more focus on polyamory scientifically.

Unlike some other aspects of identity where I could quote to you the percentage of people with 'polyamory regret', I'm not fully able to do that for you in this instance. So, in short, the answer to the simple question of whether or not polyamory is a 'phase' for your loved one is really... maybe. Because the only thing that is truly constant is change. Maybe one day I could produce figures about the actual number of people who 'go back' to monogamy. But really, I don't think that this question is, as I said, actually about that.

Stability and Failure

On a basic level, I believe the anxiety behind this question and what it's attempting to control has a lot to do with wanting stability for your loved one. A lot of people, for understandable reasons, feel comforted by the familiar and the known: the cultural script of monogamy provides us with a sign of stability. Choosing a relationship style that is not within that cultural script feels less stable, regardless of the people involved. The lack of stability makes it seem like this could be a 'phase', or there may be a fear that polyamory is not stable enough to be something that is not a 'phase'.

Through my years of giving advice, I probably have run across more negative stories than most people have and despite that, I do feel that in the process of exploring polyamory, what you consider a 'failure' really depends on how you look at it. What might be more helpful for you in addressing your anxiety about your loved one is less of a focus on reaffirming the idea that polyamory is always stable or will be stable and more of a focus on challenging the very concept of what 'stable' means and is relationships.

There is an underlying and understandable assumption that relationships are only successful if they last until someone within the relationship dies. This is something that often goes unquestioned in monogamous-centric society, though I do think we are questioning things more and more. Though we today have a society where people can get a divorce without societal exclusion, we still often see divorces and breakups as a sign of failure. Even polyamorous people reinforce this when they claim that monogamy may not work for everyone based on the 50 per cent divorce rate.

What if we decided that there are different ways to define 'success' in a relationship that don't revolve around longevity? Breakups are difficult and emotional and a good deal of us intend to be in relationships for the long haul. However, the shame people often experience at the loss of a relationship still remains. Relationships are a lot more complicated than that, though. Shorter relationships can be successful for the people involved, and staying in relationships to avoid breaking up isn't always what is actually best for all parties.

It is understandable to be concerned for your loved one and want stability and long-lasting partnerships for them. But it's important to remember that not only is it not inherently a failure to experience shorter relationships or to have a relationship end, but that monogamy in and of itself is not a guarantee of longevity. The fear behind this desire for longevity is also based on a fear of a loved one experiencing pain, which brings me to the next concept.

Preventing Pain

Understandably, we do not want our loved one to experience pain, if we can help it. To a certain extent, we do realize that there is only so much we can do to protect our loved one from the ups and downs they may experience in the world, and a few of us understand that sometimes in trying to protect our loved one from experiencing pain, we might actually cause them more problems later on down the line.

The fear lying behind the question of whether or not polyamory is a 'phase' your loved one is going through often comes from a fear of them experiencing pain. Pain in losing relationships, pain in not being accepted, pain that seems inevitable for something new, all of this. It's normal to want your child to not have to go through any more strife or difficulty than they may already have to face just living in the world. But the assumption with that is that the path of least resistance is always safer.

It's easy to assume that polyamory, if it is in fact a choice for your loved one, is always going to result in more pain and that monogamy will result in less pain. There is a logic to the idea. All relationships come to an end, or we come to an end. The more relationships you have, the higher the incidence of relationships ending and therefore, the higher the likelihood of pain. What I think people tend to forget is that monogamous people don't always have fewer relationships and polyamorous people don't always have more. If you're a serial monogamist who frequently enters into new partnerships and ends them, over time, you can end up having more relationships and more heartbreak than a polyamorous person might. The extent of pain one feels after the ending of a relationship depends on the person and situation. Not all relationships and all breakups are alike

47

or have the same impact on us. The idea that polyamory will inevitably bring your loved one more pain or heartbreak is an oversimplification of the situation.

At the end of the day, whether or not polyamory is a 'phase' for your loved one, conflict is an inevitable part of human interaction and experiencing pain is part of human existence. Recognizing that you don't have control over preventing your loved one from experiencing any pain in their life is a good step towards getting to the root of this question and what's causing you to ask it.

Validity of Our Choices

The last aspect of this question that I want to address is what validates our choices in life. What underlies this question, which I think frustrates many people, is the belief that polyamory is not really as valid a choice as monogamy is. The idea that it must be a 'phase' or a temporary thing sends the message that it's less of a real option than monogamy is. This is pretty similar to what people find offensive about the idea that being bisexual or gay is a 'phase'.

The typical counteraction towards this claim is to point to people who have been polyamorous for long periods of time to reinforce the idea that it's not a 'phase'. While I'm not necessarily against this and I know many people who have been polyamorous for a decent amount of their lives, the problem I have with this is that it reinforces the idea that we have to stick with a choice for the rest of our lives in order for that choice to be valid.

Similar to the idea that relationships have to last until someone doesn't make it out alive, we have a similar idea as to what makes a choice 'valid'. We know from history that the shame of getting a divorce in the past has kept people in painful, difficult relationships unnecessarily. Likewise, the idea that certain choices are not valid unless they are true for the rest of our lives has the power to keep people unnecessarily locked into choices that may not serve them.

If you wish to be a supportive loved one, I think it is important to provide an environment where your loved one doesn't feel they have to prove to you the validity of their choices in such a way that they end up staying in unhappy situations. Maybe polyamory is what we would describe as a 'phase', but it may still be an important part of your loved one's life that you have the power to validate in whatever form it takes. A choice doesn't have to last for the rest of our lives to be important to us or to our lives.

As someone who is a supportive loved one, I'm sure you would rather your loved one become monogamous again if that really was what they wanted rather than feeling a pressure to remain in a polyamorous relationship for the sake of proving something to you or anyone else. Regardless of what polyamory ends up being to your loved one, providing them validation of their choices even if you have your fears or reservations is one of the most powerful things you can do.

2. DID I DO SOMETHING WRONG?

This question is going to be difficult for a lot of polyamorous people to hear from a loved one because on a basic level, it is a suggestion that polyamory itself is 'wrong'. While I'm sure there are many people out there who do believe that any form of non-monogamy is wrong due to their specific definitions of morality, even those loved ones who do not have any specific moral reason to object to polyamory may still have this initial reaction towards their loved one disclosing non-monogamy to them.

While it is easy to jump towards offence when it comes to this question, if you are a loved one reading this book with the intent of learning to support your loved one best, I am going to assume that you mean no harm. There are a couple of aspects in the nuance of this question that I can suggest, even if you feel this way and aren't quite sure where it's coming from.

Normal as Safe

As I've discussed previously, there is an assumption a lot of people make, even polyamorous people during times of duress, that monogamy is a 'safer' way to go about relationships. I think a lot of loved ones, when they hear that their loved one is non-monogamous, ask if they have done something wrong because they are looking for a reason behind the panic that arises. This is the panic that many automatically experience because their loved one is going off the script of what they have been raised to believe is the best way to live life.

It's less about the idea that polyamory is 'wrong' explicitly and more about the fear of the unknown, the fear of their loved one stepping outside of the cultural script, and a very common reinforced belief that a monogamous marriage is a 'safer' option. I want to express that polyamorous people themselves have issues with breaking down this script when they are dealing with some of the ups and downs that polyamory can bring to them. When we're going against what society has told us is supposed to give us a happy, successful life, we're going to have anxiety about it.

It's unrealistic to expect a polyamorous person to have no anxiety around this and likewise unrealistic to expect family members to have no feelings about this.

If we really think about this, this initial reaction happens in so many other situations where people go off the cultural script. The idea of not being married by a certain age, the idea of not going to university, the idea of attempting to choose an arts-based job, and plenty of other situations often have loved ones in a panic over whether or not their loved one will end up destitute, miserable or unable to help themselves or live a full life. And in many situations, specifically parents choose to blame themselves or wonder what their contribution was in their loved one turning away from the trusted path.

When we discussed this previously in the book, I pointed out that the normal and trusted path is not a guarantee of happiness and I could re-emphasize that here, but when it comes to this specific emotion in terms of wondering if you've done something 'wrong', I don't think that would be helpful. I think it's unrealistic of me to tell you that your loved one will experience more love and more happiness in polyamory than they would in monogamy. The level of happiness one experiences in any given path in their life is not really predictable by anyone.

Your worry about your loved one going off script and experiencing more hardship because of it is actually very valid. But it may help you to remember that the safety that your loved one has actually comes from a supportive and caring environment, rather than the path that they take. Even if they experience more hardship on a non-monogamous path, the important part is that they have people in their life to support them emotionally. I can tell you as someone who has lacked the support of loved ones throughout my life during all periods and times that the normal here that is the most safe is not actually monogamy, it's a loving and supportive family.

The Impact of Childhood

The second part of this worry comes from the idea that the influence of the parent has had an impact on the type of path we decide to go down as adults. I am definitely not a childhood development expert. While I am learning more about the way children's brains work, and that has helped me immensely in handling my anxiety and improving my life overall, I can't sit here and tell you that your decisions as a parent definitely did or didn't have an impact on the reasons behind why your loved one has either recognized they are polyamorous or chosen non-monogamy.

The first aspect of this concept that I want to point out, however, is that by and large, the people who are concerned about the impact that they have had on their child are probably a lot better parents than they think they are. By definition, being concerned about what impact you had on your child is at least a positive step forward. But it's equally important to understand, from what little I do know about child development from experts like Gabor Maté, that being focused on being a perfect parent is an impossible standard to hold yourself to.

Parents are human beings. They experience emotional ups and downs and sometimes don't have the tools themselves to handle what life throws at them on top of also being expected to raise another human being and teach them the skills to manage their emotions and live better lives than they did. This doesn't mean that no parent is ever responsible for preventable damage they have done to their kids or that life's stressors make anything they do acceptable or okay. Nor does it mean that any adult has to accept everything about how their parents raised them.

What this does mean is that it's unreasonable to expect even a parent with the best resources and least stressful job and life to be a perfect parent all of the time. And from what little I know of child development and from my own personal childhood and relationship with my own parents, those parents that are willing to recognize their imperfections, even later on down the line, and relate to their children as best as they can are actually doing great when it comes to repairing any issues that they may have caused.

Now, I could very easily say to you, 'You think you did something wrong in childhood to cause your child to be polyamorous but being polyamorous isn't wrong so problem solved!' But I don't know if that would actually convince this inner voice that is worried that you didn't do what you should have done. It may have been something you have worried about long before polyamory came into the picture. Instead, I think the root of the problem should be addressed.

Our childhoods do have an impact on us. I don't believe that brain development and human behaviour are simple enough for anyone to say, 'Ah, you divorced your partner so you taught your child that monogamy doesn't work and that's why!' And I think anyone who offers you a seemingly simple answer to a complicated social decision is probably just giving you a false sense of security (and is likely selling something). It's simply too complicated for even the most experienced of psychotherapists to pinpoint in such simplistic terms.

There may be aspects of their childhood that made your loved one question if the social script that was sold to them is a good choice or not. This isn't actually a bad thing. Your loved one being brave enough to actually seek out what they know will make them happy, and feeling safe enough to do that, is a sign of strong self-esteem which could be equally attributed to their childhood. But at the end of the day, what has happened within the past is beyond your control. What you can change and work on is your behaviour in the present. Being concerned about the effects that you could have had on your child is an admirable trait, and it is sometimes half the battle when it comes to building a positive relationship with your loved one as an adult. Give yourself the credit that you are at least taking the steps towards that with your loved one now, regardless of what has happened in the past.

The Meaning of Commitment

An aspect of the fear that a loved one can have when they ask this question is the worry that, without following the typical cultural script that they have been told will guarantee success, their loved one may never get to have deeper relationships. When most people consider polyamory 'wrong', even unintentionally, it is with the assumption that polyamorous people cannot 'commit' and that is why they are polyamorous or that their relationship is more shallow than a traditional long-term monogamous relationship.

This is a very common misunderstanding of polyamory. I won't tell you that there aren't people out there practising what they call polyamory who aren't all that interested in establishing committed romantic relationships with others and are more interested in chasing 'new relationship energy' (NRE). I wouldn't say these people are 'afraid' of commitment and really there isn't anything wrong with chasing NRE if that's what you want. It becomes more of a problem when people are not honest with themselves or others about it.

However, the vast majority of polyamorous people, one can argue, are *so* interested in commitment that they desire to do it with more than one person. Rather than being afraid of it, most polyamorous people embrace it. The fear that polyamory doesn't lead to commitments is really contradictory to what usually happens within polyamory. In fact, in some cases I feel like people are even less obliged to break up with people because they *can* date other people.

This is again a case of questioning the script that even you were handed when it comes to what assumptions are made, not just about what it looks like to commit but also what commitment means. It makes sense that many of us seek out longer-term commitments and obviously want our relationships to last for a long time, but commitments are not guarantees. Even if your loved one is not necessarily seeking out multiple long-term commitments, or they do seek them out and do not find them, it doesn't mean they will be miserable or unhappy.

Open your mind to the different types of commitments and different ways that they might present in your loved one's life and don't assume that going through ups and downs of relationships is a sign of failure.

Polyamory Isn't Wrong

Last but not least, and maybe I don't need to tell you this if you're interested enough to read this book, polyamory isn't objectively a 'wrong' choice for anyone to make. It may be the wrong choice for your loved one, sure. But that is something they will have to figure out on their own. In and of itself, it isn't a 'wrong' choice. And even though it feels like a new thing, it's not necessarily any newer than the concept of leaning into romantic love.

One of the fallacies a lot of people end up falling into when talking about human social behaviour is the idea of what is 'traditional' or 'natural'. It's easy for us to believe that monogamous marriage, especially within the context of the stereotypical 'nuclear' family, is the way family structures have been for a long time throughout human societies, but even a cursory examination of this over the last couple of hundreds of years would show it to not be true.

In a fantastic paper on the myth of the 'male breadwinner', Rebecca Sear notes that concepts of the traditionality of the 'nuclear' family emerged after the Second World War but that historically, evidence shows that family units consisted of pair bonds but also the involvement of other adults including grandparents; as the saying goes, 'It takes a village'. There are lots of ways ideas of the 'traditional' are reinforced by our society that come to us as second nature which are not in fact nature at all (Sear, 2021).

Romantic love has not always been seen as a valid thing worth exploring. I'm sure many people are more than aware of the history of marriage as a social contract or the exchange of property, which women were once considered to be, rather than a sign of eternal commitment and undying devotion. In many cases, throughout history, men, especially those with social power, have had the power to seek whatever relationships outside of their official 'marriage'. There are lots of ways we have renegotiated what romantic love means, what coupledom means, what partnership means and what the family means throughout history.

Polyamory may be a new name, but it is not necessarily a completely new concept and, even if it is a uniquely new concept, it isn't necessarily a 'wrong' way to go. It may just be a different way to pursue what humans have been pursuing for years now: connection and togetherness. This introduction to polyamory via your loved one may give you the permission you need to question concepts of 'tradition' that have kept you from finding your own bliss in life.

3. ARE THEY BEING PUSHED INTO THIS?

There are a variety of ways that people get into polyamory. There may be some people who are alive now and of dating age who have grown up with polyamory, but the vast majority of people will be exposed to non-monogamy well after they begin to date. A good deal of people will already be within a monogamous relationship when they discover that non-monogamy is a possibility for them.

Some people will be introduced to non-monogamy through their partner asking for it within their relationship. Sometimes it happens through cheating or infidelity and other times it happens because there are relationship problems and a belief that opening the relationship is the solution to those problems.

Ideally, everyone would know as early as they know monogamy is a choice that polyamory is also a choice so they can consider it outside of a situation where they may lose a relationship. But realistically, that is not the way most people will be introduced to it. With that context, it makes sense that you as a loved one might be worried about your loved one being 'pushed' into polyamory within an already established relationship, especially if it was not originally their idea.

Anxiety Is Normal

Throughout the years of giving advice both in public forums and within my own column and podcast, a good deal of my efforts involves encouraging people to see their emotions as normal. The vast majority of people starting off in polyamory will feel an enormous pressure to 'prove that polyamory works' to both themselves and the rest of the world.

Even if your loved one is not the one who introduced polyamory into their relationship, or even if they are not dating anyone and they have decided this is a path they want to go down, there is an enormous combination of pressures on them. They are trying a new way of doing relationships that they have no social script for, which is causing their brain to freak out a bit, and then on top of that there is, unlike with monogamy, the chance that they can't 'do polyamory' and they may find out the hard way.

It is for this reason that I think it is extremely normal for people to experience anxiety when starting out in polyamory. If you add that to the pressure of trying to keep an existing relationship alive and whatever issues have been going on in that relationship, then it's an enormous amount of pressure to make things 'work'. While to the best of my knowledge this hasn't been studied, it would not be surprising to me if the stress of switching a relationship style was equal to the amount of stress of a big move, a divorce, death of a spouse, job shift and any of the other major life stressors.

All of this is to say that if you notice your loved one is anxious about polyamory, this isn't necessarily a sign that they were pushed into polyamory or that it wasn't a good choice for them. You as a loved one have the ability to either contribute to that stress or make that stress lighter. It makes sense for you to be worried about your loved one, but seeing every anxiety they have as a sign they were 'pushed into' polyamory may be pushing them away from you instead.

Polyamory Under Duress

There are many reasons why your loved one is either trying polyamory without having an interest in it or finally allowing themselves to try something they have wanted to try all along but if it comes as a surprise to you, then it may be difficult for you, especially if they are in a monogamous relationship, to believe they are not being pushed into it in some way. And I would be lying to you if I said that there were no situations where people are trying polyamory to avoid a breakup or doing what we call 'polyamory under duress'.

There is a nuance to our decisions in life that can not always be captured or understood by people standing outside of them. I have often encouraged people to avoid trying polyamory in order to 'save' their relationship. In the same way I wouldn't advise someone to go a long distance to 'save' a relationship if they could not do long distance, I would equally not advise polyamory to 'save' a relationship, because the relationship you are trying to save will be functionally different.

However, realistically, many people will try polyamory because they don't want to break up with their partner, even if they don't really want to do it. I don't believe that every single one of these situations can be described as 'polyamory under duress' because I think that relationships and the things we decide to do are much more complicated than that. All relationships in our lives involve compromise and sometimes doing things we aren't absolutely enthusiastically positive about doing.

If you agreed to sit down with your partner for ten hours and watch all three extended editions of The Lord of the Rings even though you're not really that into it, that isn't The Lord of the Rings Under Duress. You might feel some duress at the seventh hour of the marathon, sure, but it's not the same as being forced. However, if your partner said they would not speak to you any more unless you watched all three extended editions of The Lord of the Rings with them, that would be a different type of duress.

Introducing polyamory to a monogamous relationship – even the idea of it – can be an absolute deal breaker. It's one of those things where either you do it or you don't. There are very few ways to 'compromise' on polyamory and so it can be difficult for the actual ask to *not* be 'I want to do this and if you don't, we have to break up', even if that's not how you want to introduce polyamory. If you are the one to introduce it, I believe you have a responsibility to be the one to walk away if you feel it's something you need and your partner cannot do.

However, there are some people who will basically force their partner to be the one to make the decision to end the relationship by either telling them that they are going to 'do polyamory anyway' (or cheat, basically) or tell them that they might break up with them if they don't agree to doing polyamory. This is specifically polyamory under duress and it is not something that most of the polyamory communities I have been in think is acceptable or ethical.

I am guessing if your loved one gave you this book, it is not likely they are actually under duress. However, the important part of this as well as the original question is to understand one basic truth – if your loved one *is* being 'pushed into' polyamory, then having another force in their life that is using the threat of losing a relationship to get them to do something is not an answer. If they are already under duress, putting them under even more duress is not really the answer.

I Told You So Crowd

If your loved one is someone who has decided to do polyamory and it wasn't something that they chose for themselves, they are already facing an enormous amount of stress in both trying to shift to a new relationship style and also maintaining their current relationship. Just because your loved one wasn't the one to introduce the concept doesn't necessarily mean it is doomed to failure or that is a bad thing.

When non-monogamous relationships don't end up working out, there is an added shame many people face because of the cultural reinforcement that open relationships 'don't work'. Even if people no longer have any interest in non-monogamy, they might still hide their relationship failure so they don't have to hear everyone else reinforce the cultural idea that it doesn't work, which inevitably sends the message that the pain the person is going through is self-caused.

Chances are if you have been given this book, your loved one has enough confidence in their choice or their relationship to tell you because you aren't going to be part of the 'told you so crowd' if their relationships don't end up working out the way they hope for. However, they may still feel a reasonable amount of trepidation in disclosing to you some of the anxieties they feel during their experience because of the fear of judgement or that this will be seen as 'proof'.

The question of whether or not your loved one is being 'pushed into' polyamory can contribute towards you being part of the 'told you so' crowd. While your fear may be coming from a reasonable place in wanting to make sure your loved one isn't in a bad situation, if they do feel pushed into trying polyamory, even if they aren't under duress, asking this question can make them feel like they can never come back and admit that they weren't as enthusiastic about it as they thought they were.

Especially if your loved one is not under duress but is still a little bit unsure if polyamory is for them, a commitment on your part to the idea that they are being forced into it may make them feel like they now have to stick to polyamory in order to prove you wrong in a way. There are already a lot of reasons your loved one may feel like they have to stick it out, even if it isn't actually something they want to do. Sometimes being part of that 'I told you so' crowd contributes to the pressure to stick it out rather than helping anyone who is actually being pushed into it.

Communities and Isolation

Trying something that isn't part of your cultural script or isn't part of what most people do can be exciting and new but it can also be incredibly isolating. Monogamous people can confide in their family and friends about their relationships without having the very nature of the way they do their relationships challenged or questioned. They don't have to have basic conversations or educate someone about how their relationships work while also dealing with the added stress that's in their lives.

Polyamory communities can be great resources for polyamorous people to talk about their relationships and what's happening within them. But not every single person has a community they can rely on or reach out to and building relationships with other people takes time that not every single person has. And that pressure to show the world that polyamory 'works' or that your loved one can 'do' polyamory sometimes is intensified rather than relieved within communities.

There is a reason why people in abusive relationships are often encouraged by the people abusing them to separate from their families or their friends. Abusive people will often cause problems by either starting fights, spreading rumours, or insisting that family members or friends are a bad influence or even abusive themselves. The intention is usually to cause a rift between the support network and the person they are abusing so that they have nowhere else but the abusive person to run to. Many polyamorous people are already cut off and isolated from support networks because they do not feel they can tell their loved ones about being polyamorous or even discuss what is happening in their relationships with their loved ones.

I can't tell you for sure if your loved one is being 'pushed into' polyamory. But I can tell you for sure that if they are being pushed into and experiencing polyamory under duress, what they need more than anything else are loved ones who support and care for them no matter what happens. While I know that this question is not intended to isolate and alienate a loved one, it can sometimes end up doing that.

It's incredibly important for loved ones to provide a space for their loved one to land softly, no matter what happens to them. I think even if you have asked your polyamorous loved one this question out of fear, you can still go back and reassure them that there is no judgement on your part and that you aren't just sitting back and waiting for polyamory to blow up in their face.

They may still not feel like they can discuss some of the anxieties they are feeling with you because they wouldn't do that in monogamy anyway, but you can at least make sure they are not totally isolated in what they are going through.

4. WHY CAN'T THEY JUST BE MONOGAMOUS?

Parents or loved ones might feel a combination of stress and confusion when their loved one tells them that they are polyamorous. None of this comes from a negative place, even though it might lead to a negative place. Generally speaking, I think that if a parent or loved one cares enough to be asking questions or to be involved in their loved one's life, that's an extremely good start. However, this question, as much as it comes from a place of frustration and confusion, may be a lot more hurtful than the previous questions.

Without intending it, the implication of this question for a polyamorous person is that the default is monogamy and that polyamory is always a choice. If your loved one feels that polyamory is an inherent part of who they are, it can feel especially invalidating to have a loved one suggest they can just choose to be monogamous. The wider point to this, however, is that even if polyamory is a choice for your loved one, suggesting that it is a negative choice can come with some pain. Assuming you don't mean to cause your loved one any pain, we'll break down the thought process behind this question.

Making a Choice

There are two aspects to this question that it proposes that are worth thinking through. The first is the implication that our relationship styles are a specific choice we're making. Some people feel as though polyamory is an inherent part of who they are. Personally, I don't necessarily think that it is useful to argue with people about things they feel are inherent parts of who they are. On a basic level, we're social creatures and we require social relationships to properly function. Part of those social relationships involves understanding ourselves and being able to explain ourselves to others.

Labels are things that help us process our identities and explain them quickly to others. Most of our social identities are socially constructed concepts – which doesn't make them any less important in our lives. As we get older, I think the labels that we tend to hold onto become a little less important because some of our relationships in our lives feel a lot more stable. You may be at a point in your life where you feel a little bit more secure in who you are than your loved one does, so the labels that you once used for yourself are less important to you now than they once were. For your loved one, the identity of being polyamorous, whether they feel it is a choice or not, is important enough for them to tell you.

Focusing on an idea that something is a choice from the standpoint of a parent, family member or loved one who is trying to understand someone polyamorous misses the point entirely. Whether or not polyamory is a choice your loved one is making, the decision to tell you or not and to let you into that part of their life was definitely a choice. They made that choice because they wanted you to see a part of them that they could have hidden from you completely. The effort they are making is to include you in their life in the best way they can when they could have chosen to keep you out.

I could go into an analysis of why polyamory isn't a bad choice to make, why it's valid, why it's something that, if it is a choice, is absolutely fine to choose, but the more important aspect here is that your loved one is including you in a part of who they are. While polyamory isn't necessarily widely known enough for individuals to feel that there is a high likelihood of their family disowning them for being polyamorous, there is enough unknown around the identity that it makes sense for your loved one to have more than a little trepidation around telling you.

Focus a little less on whether or not your loved one could change their identity and recognize that they have let you into a part of them and this is a sign that your relationship is getting closer rather than further apart.

Importance of Validation

As I've previously mentioned, human beings are social creatures. We thrive in social relationships. The validation that our loved ones can provide us is fundamentally critical in multiple aspects of our lives. Although polyamory is not the same as sexual orientation, we have a lot of documented evidence that having at least one accepting adult lowers the rate of suicidality in the lives of LGBTQ youth, according to a 2023 report from The Trevor Project (Trevor Project, 2023).

Loved ones are in a particularly strong position to help and provide support for anyone in any group, especially if they are likely to feel alone. According to the National Alliance on Mental

Illness, family members and caregivers play a large role in providing support for people with mental health conditions (National
Alliance on Mental Illness, n.d.). While obviously polyamory is
not a mental health condition, the stress of following the least
trodden path can sometimes be quite overwhelming.

I think those supporting a polyamorous loved one may feel
frustrated by the challenges that they see coming down a path
that is less defined. Loved ones feel like this is simply a choice
that their polyamorous loved one could solve by just choosing a
different path. Whether or not your loved one sees polyamory
as an inherent part of who they are, your ability to provide them
with support especially if they are reaching out for it is incredibly
important.

The frustration you may feel is something that I believe you
can express, just not necessarily to your loved one directly. If you
can find someone else such as a therapist or use a free listening
service to help you express some of your feelings, this might
help you work through some of your emotions. Expressing these
directly to your loved one while they are struggling with needing
your support and validation, even if you don't intend for your
words to hurt, can be incredibly difficult.

Many times people also wish to fully *understand* their loved
one and that often stands in the way of providing validation –
almost as if you have to fully understand someone before you
can really validate them. While I understand that we all want to
fully understand our loved ones, sometimes fully understanding
an experience just isn't possible and the effort to try and 'get'
polyamory can actually get in the way. Let go of the idea that you
have to fully understand every aspect of polyamory before you
can provide needed validation.

At some point you may indeed understand polyamory slightly

more than you did before. But this may take a little bit of time. In the meantime, being there for your loved one is the most important support you can provide for them.

Veering Off the Cultural Script

For this section, let's assume that polyamory is fully and completely a choice in the same way that other aspects of our lifestyles can be choices. One similar choice that a lot of loved ones may be concerned about is the choice to not have children or to be intentionally child-free. This is a more well known lifestyle choice, which loved ones tend to have some reasonable emotions about.

Being child-free comes with a lot of cultural baggage, and is still veering off of the cultural script that many are told is required for future happiness. Though a small and limited study, in 2022 researchers at the Michigan State University found no conclusive evidence to support a high prevalence of regret among people actively choosing to be childfree – one of the most common misconceptions about being child-free (Dolan, 2023).

Not being able to have children and wanting them is a situation many unfortunately find themselves in, but this is different to people who actively *choose* to be child-free. This is arguably and definitely a choice, but this doesn't make this any less of a valid way to live. But parents who imagined themselves being grandparents may feel like their loved one's choice to not have children definitely has an impact on their lives, and the truth is that it does in some way.

The emotions a parent may feel at the news that they will never become a grandparent *are* valid emotions, while the lifestyle choices of their loved one are also valid. When examining this situation objectively, we don't have to choose who is 'more right' in their emotions. We can appreciate the nuance of the situation and hold a space for all perspectives and emotions. Given that being child-free is a little better known than polyamory, you may also, as a loved one, understand that it may not be fully appropriate to tell your loved one directly about the emotions you have around this.

Being child-free can sometimes create obstacles in people's lives depending on their social circles, but many people have a variety of reasons for choosing to be child-free and polyamory is fairly similar. Just because something we choose can sometimes create obstacles for us doesn't mean that the choice itself isn't the right choice for us. In both cases, just choosing what seems like the path of least resistance is actually a path of greater resistance.

Even as you as a loved one may experience emotions around the choice of being child-free, in that situation many would understand that the decision to have a child is something permanent and long-lasting. While polyamory as a choice may not necessarily be identical to that choice, deciding to try and go along with a monogamous relationship can often become more or less a permanent decision. Our time is our most precious resource and the time we spend living a lifestyle we don't really want is time that is permanently lost.

Considering the Other Party

Another aspect of the situation that is worth considering that I find many loved ones asking this question don't consider is the future and the life of the individual who would end up in a monogamous relationship with your loved one. In the heat of the moment, if you have asked this question, what's going through your mind is a happy future with your loved one happily existing and supported in a monogamous relationship.

It would be extremely unlikely that your loved one would end up with another polyamorous person who was also choosing to be monogamous for the sake of their family or loved ones. It's more likely that your loved one would end up in a relationship with a person who was not interested in polyamory. In so many of my advice columns and podcasts and in forums I see a constant stream of people already in monogamous relationships where they discover that polyamory is more suited for them and are faced with the monumental task of having to tell their partner or face a lifetime of unhappiness and 'what ifs'.

For the individual on the opposite side of this equation, there is an equally monumental decision: to try polyamory to save their relationship, or end it. Despite the fact that I think it is often easier to end a relationship than to try and fit a square peg in a round hole, I equally can't blame people, especially those who have already spent years in their current relationship, and have children or financial ties together, if they want to save their connection in any way possible.

It's a difficult and rough ride – and it may be the situation that your loved one is currently in or considering. The happiness in this fantasy exists in both your loved one and their monogamous partner. But consider this reality: It is unlikely that your loved one is going to end up with someone else who is also polyamorous, but pretending to be monogamous for the sake of their family. It's more likely that, if they force themselves to be in a monogamous relationship, it will be with someone who is monogamous themselves. If there is one thing that I think monogamous and polyamorous people have in common it is that we want our partners to be happy.

Most of us would not want our partners to be living a lie, secretly unhappy for years on end and only pretending to be happy for the sake of avoiding a breakup or meeting our familial expectations – though this was realistically how many people lived before divorce was socially acceptable, and still how many people who struggle to accept their own identities in a variety of ways live today. Equally, I think most of us would not want to believe that our partner was happy in a relationship when they weren't.

So it's worth asking yourself to consider the person your partner would be with if they decided to 'just be monogamous'. Would that person be with a person who is happy or who is just pretending to be happy? Is it fair to that person to spend years and years with someone who is secretly unhappy when they could spend that time finding someone who would actually be happy with them? It's easy to be laser focused on your loved one in these situations, but the reality is that there is another party involved in this equation who could potentially end up living a lie with them.

There are a lot of understandable feelings behind this question and a lot of fears that make sense, but rather than using this section to validate polyamory and show its value as a good 'choice', I think it is important to show you the value you bring to your loved one through your support. Because the truth is, I can't tell you if polyamory *is* a good choice for your loved one, or even if it is a choice at all for them. But I can tell you that whether or not they end up monogamous, they will need your support, understanding and love regardless.

71

5. DON'T THEY FEEL INADEQUATE?

The background cultural script of monogamy includes some pretty commonly reinforced lines. In Billboard's top 50 love songs, all but one of the top five songs include some line which reinforces exclusivity and the concept that your partner meets all of your needs (Bronson, 2024). If you listen to the lyrics of these songs, you will find lines that reinforce exclusivity, such as saying that nobody else is suitable and suggesting that love should be given all to one person:

- Endless Love by Diana Ross and Lionel Richie
- How Deep Is Your Love by the Bee Gees
- We Found Love by Rihanna featuring Calvin Harris
- Silly Love Songs by Wings.

While this is a small sample, I'm sure if you reviewed your own favourite love songs, you'd see multiple principles reinforced including the idea that there is only one perfect person for everyone, that the one person who is perfect will meet all your needs, that your eyes shouldn't wander if the one you love is perfect for you, and that there is a perfection that your partner meets that can't be surpassed by anyone else.

A society that encourages us to consume and purchase as much as possible has every motivation to reinforce this idea. We have a desire to find love and social connection and believing one must be a certain way, look a certain way, or do a certain thing in order to find that love is something that companies use to sell us things constantly and it only further reinforces the idea that *you* should be 'adequate' enough to find a partner.

Is it then that unexpected that you would assume that

wanting more than one partner represents an inadequacy some-where? Not really, when you think about it.

Meeting Needs

One of the things polyamorous people hear a lot about and which may have been passed along to you is the idea that one person can't meet everyone's needs. I think this philosophy comforts people who have found monogamy to be lacking in their life and want an explanation for that emptiness that makes sense to them. But this explanation can ring a little empty in the ears of loved ones who feel they have been in satisfying and happy monogamous relationships for years or even decades.

This philosophy is coming under some scrutiny because peo-ple have realized that seeing individuals as essentially need-meet-ing machines isn't necessarily an accurate reflection of the way people do relationships, and it's not the best way to approach relationships. Despite the idea of one perfect partner being promoted in the love songs I mentioned and the fairy tales we grew up with, the idea that one partner should fit us perfectly like a puzzle piece is not necessarily a good way to approach relationships.

There are a lot of monogamous people who end up believing they should be able to find someone who they never get into any disagreement with or get annoyed by, and this ends up harming them in the long run in their relationships. Our relationships and our needs are complicated, and there are things we can negotiate and things we can't negotiate. Relationships are complex and it's not always as simple as ticking off every single box.

Your loved one's decision to be polyamorous, to own their

polyamorous identity or to try polyamory isn't about whether or not they are adequate enough for their partner or whether or not their partner is adequate enough for them. This concept is really based on the idea that one person should be an absolute perfect fit and if they are not, then the eye goes wandering when really the situation is more complicated than that.

Different relationships can fill different needs that we have and not all needs have to be specifically met within a romantic relationship. Being over-reliant on a single romantic partner for all of your needs has consequences for monogamous people and their relationships that are not necessarily beneficial, especially if one loses their partner through death or divorce. A systematic review of the impact of social isolation on behavioural health published in 2015 reported that not only do older adults report experiencing social isolation but that social isolation affects health; specifically, the perception of a lack of social network is associated with sleep disturbances and depression (Choi et al., 2015).

It would benefit most people to expand their social circle and challenge the idea that one person should meet every single need for a variety of reasons. Summing up a decision to open a relationship as a sign of inadequacy is an oversimplification of what is behind a deeper decision your loved one is making.

Top of the Pack

The other element within the concept of 'adequacy' is an idea that's frequently reinforced in our social scripts: the concept of competition. We're encouraged to 'compete' for partners through a variety of social reinforcements. The rating system we often give people (e.g. calling someone a 10 or considering yourself 'out of their league') reinforces the idea that acquiring a partner is about competition. Countless magazines offer tips and tricks to attract and keep a partner.

While the extent of how much stock people place in this concept varies depending on the person, even polyamorous people who are actively and enthusiastically interested in polyamory can sometimes feel a nervousness about being replaced by a 'better' partner or feel nervous if one of their partners is dating someone who they see as 'better' in some way than they are at any given thing. This isn't an easy idea to let go of because some of it has a basis in truth.

While, yes, it's not as simple as someone 'winning' us like a prize, most of us do seek a partner with a certain level of communication skills and abilities and often do decline others we may find attractive because they don't have the relational skills we feel we need to make a successful relationship. While relationships themselves are a collaboration between the people involved, people can contribute nothing to that collaboration or tank that collaboration with behaviours that don't facilitate working together. As they say, there is no I in 'team', but we've all probably been on a team with someone who was not contributing and had to pull their dead weight.

Still, there are billions of people on the planet and it's impossible for one person to be excellent at everything in life. No matter whom you meet, you will find someone who is 'better' than you in any given thing that you could pick. While I'm sure there are people who are shallow enough to choose their partners as if every human being is directly comparable, most of us don't really find ourselves comparing people in such a way. We may know from previous experiences what we do and don't want in relationships and make comparisons based on that, but it's not as simple as one person winning you as a prize.

Rethinking this concept could be beneficial for almost everyone, especially younger people who still feel there are 'leagues' people exist in and that they do not have a partner because they are not 'good enough'. The reasons we are attracted to people are complex and so assuming that your loved one has somehow failed to 'beat' other people or that their partner has failed to 'beat' competition is a misunderstanding of how most people do relationships.

Social Relationships and 'Enough'

Do you make new friends because your current friendships are inadequate? If you have more than one child, you didn't have more than one because one was inadequate. In no other form of relationship are we encouraged to believe that being interested in others is a sign of inadequacy. This isn't to say that there is anything wrong with wanting a single romantic partner in the same way there isn't anything wrong with wanting one child. But our drive to expand our social relationships is not a sign that the current social relationships we have are not 'enough'.

As I said previously, given the narrative we're fed about the way real, strong and everlasting love is supposed to last, it's not surprising that a good deal of people struggle with the concept that wanting or seeking a new relationship represents an inadequacy in your current relationship. If you don't have children of your own, then imagining your friendships is a good way to put yourself in the position of a polyamorous loved one when it comes to the 'inadequacy' of relationships.

Imagine trying to compare two of your friendships, the closest ones that you have. Comparing those two friendships directly might be really difficult for you to do. There are aspects of the friendships you might be able to compare but really, two different people might exist in completely different ways in your life. I think comparing partners as complete people is like comparing apples and oranges. Different relationships are different. At times, I can definitely see where one person has stronger skills in one area than another – for sure. But this isn't at all about one person being 'inadequate'.

Even if your loved one is participating in some form of hierarchy, this doesn't necessarily represent who is 'adequate' and who is 'inadequate', though that can be easy to assume. Just as there might be friends that you would love to go to concerts with but others who wouldn't enjoy it, there are different types of partnerships that have different ways of bonding and relating that aren't as simple as one being 'enough' and one being 'not enough'.

There are lots of ways that challenging this misconception could benefit monogamous people in their own relationships. A lot of people struggle with juggling the attention they need to give to multiple relationships in their lives and some of the relational issues people have get chalked up to not being 'good enough'. Especially when people experience breakups or end up being actually replaced by others, they very much feel like they haven't been 'enough'. Only in a few cases where people are exceptionally shallow is this actually the case.

Opening a Relationship to Address an Issue

Although I have talked extensively about how it's not as simple as being inadequate, there are some cases where people are motivated to open their relationship because of an incompatibility in their current relationship. There are conflicting opinions about whether or not this is a good idea. I'm very much a proponent of the idea that one shouldn't use polyamory to avoid a breakup, and a lot of other people think the same: just as one shouldn't have a baby to solve relationship problems, adding more people to the mix won't solve relationship problems either.

For me, what determines whether this is a good approach or not lies within the complexities of the relationship as it stands and how satisfying it is. It is fully possible to have a satisfying, wonderful monogamous relationship but want to open the relationship because there is something else that you want to experience and have it work out well. Regardless of the reasonings and motivations behind why your loved one opened their relationship, and if they *did* open for the sake of addressing an issue or an incompatibility within their current relationship, it's important to remember that an incompatibility doesn't necessarily reflect inadequacy.

It is actually supremely rare for us to find a partner who fits every single aspect of the things that we want from a partner and whom we never have any disagreements with. Conflict is pretty inevitable in all relationships and small incompatibilities are pretty par for the course for many relationships. Given that, it is likely that you have experienced a relationship where you haven't been completely and utterly compatible with your partner on every measurable level. Perhaps none of these have been things that have made you want to pursue opening your relationship, or maybe you have not considered it to be a viable option for yourself. But you can understand what might lead someone into exploring other options instead of ending a relationship whenever faced with incompatibility.

It's unlikely that your loved one is going to want to discuss the innermost aspects of their relationship with you and that probably is not something they necessarily need you for. In the worst-case scenario where they are trying polyamory just to save their relationship and aren't really interested in polyamory per se, the biggest thing they will need from their support network is less judgement than they will likely see elsewhere in the world and more love and kindness.

While it makes sense that you would ask these questions, and I don't think you're necessarily trying to come from a judgemental place, it's important to understand that there are more complexities to partner choice and relationships than we have been told by the culture that we've grown up in. This is definitely one of those questions that's worth working through with a polyamory-friendly therapist, and discussing further if you find yourself coming back to it again and again. The one thing that is absolutely certain is that your loved one needs your support and love, regardless of where they are in this process.

6. DOES THEIR PARTNER REALLY LOVE THEM?

This question can be particularly harsh for a polyamorous person to hear because, again, there is a suggestion of invalidation here that a loved one may not intend when they actually ask this question. I think most loved ones ask this question because they are concerned that their polyamorous loved one may be being 'used' and are trying to protect them.

There are other questions related to the idea of whether or not your loved one is being loved adequately, such as asking about which partner is the most 'important' or which one they would choose. Sometimes this is asked out of the same concerns whereas other times there is an element of curiosity there. Hopefully this section can help quell both of these issues and help you understand a little bit more about what's going on with your polyamorous loved one.

What Is Love?

When people are opening up their relationships or starting off in polyamory, a lot of people are told the concept that 'love is infinite'. Many people think they are polyamorous purely because they have the capability to feel romantic attraction to more than one person at a time, which speaks to what our strong cultural conceptions are around romantic love.

To put it plainly, culturally we perceive romantic love as a finite resource, which is one of the reasons why polyamorous people say, 'love is infinite'. Romantic love is something we're only supposed to have for one person and if we have any type of romantic or sexual feelings for anyone else, then it means that the love we have for that person *can't* be that strong. It is a resource that we can only divide among people. This is so ingrained into people that it feels natural.

Despite the fact that in the past romantic love was seen as a sickness, or as a less valuable love than other forms of love, when we do have romantic relationships we're encouraged to prioritize them over other forms of relationships to the point where almost everyone has a story of a friend who entered into a new relationship and pretty much fell off the face of the earth in terms of communication.

Given this cultural script, it is not surprising that you would be concerned about whether or not your loved one is being loved well enough. I actually believe that most monogamous people have absolutely had moments where they have had romantic or sexual attraction to more than one person and I believe it's actually highly unrealistic to expect yourself to only ever be attracted to one person for the rest of your life. So there probably are situations where you could empathize with your polyamorous loved one in terms of having feelings for more than one person.

But if you have never had that experience, it can be a little odd for you to put yourself in the shoes of your loved one. However, you don't *have* to fully understand the real-life experience of your loved one to respect what's going on with them. At the end of the day, whether your loved one feels inherently polyamorous or not, trust their own judgement of the situation that they're in.

I can't tell you whether all people are able to love more than one person at once, but I can tell you that many, many people are not only capable of doing it but also feel more fulfilled and happy in their lives when they are able to do so. Trust that your loved one knows how to find their own happiness and challenge the inherent assumption you may have had from the cultural script you have been raised in that love is only something that you can feel for one person.

Curiosity and Questions

When people encounter a new way of living or a different way of going about something that has seemed pretty ubiquitous across humanity, they can have a negative response and fear what they don't know, or they can have a curiosity to understand it better. Overall, I feel like having a curiosity and a desire to know more about polyamory is generally a positive thing for a loved one, and certainly much better than outright rejection or disdain.

However, there is sometimes a tension involved between a loved one and a polyamorous person when that curiosity bubbles over, and the issue is that no one's emotions here are necessarily 'wrong'. If you have a huge curiosity and want to know more, you may just ask questions that you have no context for but that you want to know the answer to. Then your loved one may feel a pressure to answer your questions while at the same time feeling slightly objectified by them and struggle to maintain a balance between keeping their composure and their reasonable frustration with your questions.

Again, no one here is essentially wrong. You just are coming from completely different cultural contexts. This is where those questions of 'who do you pick first?' or 'who do you love more?' can emerge. You as a loved one are trying to understand polyamory from a monogamous-centric context, where your questions and concerns may be understandable. However, your loved one is living in a context where they may have already had to answer these questions more than once or they feel as though they need to justify polyamory to you.

Telling a loved one about something like polyamory can already be a stressful experience. Unless you have had discussions about this previously, they may fear that disclosing this to you may cause a rift or a complete break in the relationship. Emotionally, your loved one may be tapped out already by the idea of telling you. Even if you react well initially, they may fear, based on your follow-up questions, that you might at some point decide to disengage.

You may not feel this way as a loved one, but this is actually a charged situation where it can feel like you hold the power *over* your polyamorous loved one. After all, they are being incredibly vulnerable and risking the loss of their relationship with you. You have the power in that instance to continue the relationship or to reject them. Until things cool down a little, they may feel very vulnerable.

While I think it's understandable to want to ask a bunch of questions about polyamory, if your loved one has just opened up to you about being polyamorous it may not exactly be the best time to begin asking these types of questions. Because your loved one might feel that they could give you the wrong impression of polyamory or somehow make you upset by answering questions 'wrong', it's not a good time to be innately curious about poly-amory in general.

Obviously, not all polyamorous people are identical and your mileage may vary when it comes to your polyamorous loved one. They may have no issue with answering questions right away and you may have the type of relationship where deeply personal questions or curiosity are no problem for them or not emotion-ally taxing, but this is not always the case. I don't say this to mean you have to walk on eggshells around your polyamorous loved one. But I say this to encourage you to be aware of your curiosity and patient with what you want to know. Check in with your loved one and ask if they are in a place where they can answer your questions before you let your curiosity take hold completely.

Hierarchies and Time

Your concern about whether or not your polyamorous loved one is being 'really loved' by their partner, or if they really love their partners, may also come from observing a hierarchy in relationships. If your partner is married or in an established relationship, it might be difficult for you to feel that they are being completely loved if their partner is interested in dating others, or you may have a reasonable expectation that whoever is married or in a more established or physically enmeshed relationship, this represents a stronger bond.

There are a variety of reasons for why polyamorous people choose different types of relationship structures. And since there are so many different types of relationships and polyamorous people in them, there may exist a situation out there where someone organizes their relationship hierarchically based upon the depth of feeling they have for their individual partners – though I would say based on my experiences, that would be a pretty unusual thing for a polyamorous person to say.

One thing I can say for sure is that a hierarchy doesn't reflect how deeply someone feels for someone else. I don't blame loved ones for being confused by this because a lot of people starting off in polyamory get confused about it. Love is infinite, but time is not infinite. We have a limited amount of time and energy we can put into different relationships. Some people only have the mental headspace for two relationships in their lives and others have more space.

A lot of people insist that they don't have any hierarchies in place when, even if they don't have an *emotional* hierarchy in place, they still automatically allocate more of their time and energy to some partners than others. They love all of their partners in a very similar way and don't feel one is 'better' than the other. That is legitimate, but I often tell polyamorous people that almost all of us have some sort of hierarchy of time and energy. We choose who we give our time and energy to based on a variety of things. And if we have children, they are usually at the top of our time hierarchy.

As a loved one, it's important for you to understand that any hierarchy your polyamorous loved one is part of or has in their life doesn't come from a place of loving someone less or being loved less. For example, if you have multiple children and one is a teenager and one is a newborn, you will likely give the newborn more of your physical time because they need it. This isn't about loving your other children less, but about an allocation of time.

With a mono-centric cultural script, we're encouraged to prioritize our romantic relationship over all other relationships. I often feel that this is not a good thing for monogamous people to do and it's actually quite important for us to give some of our time to both our friendships and our family members rather than just getting completely consumed by a new romantic relationship.

However, given this script it would make sense that you as a loved one would see a hierarchy as a sign of a 'lesser' love. Just try to keep in mind that the time that people spend on specific relationships is not reflective of the amount of love they have for that person.

Control and Assumptions

There are some polyamorous people who believe that monogamy is inherently controlling. While I don't believe that is true, I do believe that sometimes the standards that a monogamous-centric culture can push people towards can feel very controlling. If we think about the most popular love songs I referenced previously, those and many others include concepts that involve owning each other's hearts, belonging to each other, and, as many people are familiar with, their partner being 'their better half'.

Often, I think these types of comments are rhetoric, and not designed to be taken literally or with any amount of seriousness, but there are other times I wonder if this is really the case. Peppered throughout culture is a narrative of 'catching' and 'keeping' a partner, especially for single people, and I think this definitely reinforces the idea that monogamy is 'controlling'. As a loved one who is likely to be monogamous, you may not feel like you need to challenge this type of ownership rhetoric because it becomes more of an issue when there are multiple partners. You may even find joy in this type of rhetoric – and that's okay!

This isn't just about loving more than one person at once. There are some people who may never find themselves in that position, and you don't have to be in that position in order to understand an underlying concept: as much as we want to keep our loved ones in our lives and as much as we all wish, within reason, to avoid a breakup, if we love someone truly with all of our hearts, then we want them to be happy. I believe that most of us feel that way about our loved ones.

As much as we love and care for people, we wouldn't want them to be living an unhappy life with us just for the sake of us being happy. I don't think people have a desire in monogamy to control their partners and, deep down, the vast majority of people wouldn't want their partners to stay with them if they were unhappy or not in love with them. I often remind polyamorous people who are scared of losing their partners that there is only so much they can do to prevent their partners from falling out of love with them.

So instead of trying to understand how your loved one can love more than one person at once or how their partner can love more than one person at once, understand that we can't actually control who we or the ones we love fall in love with, and *we wouldn't want to control it.* If anyone could control who they fell in love with, there would be a lot less relationship issues in monogamy or polyamory. Either way, most of us care about our partners being happy.

If we could essentially force our partners to stay in love with us forever, regardless of what they want in life, most of us would consider that unethical and would not want to do that to our loved ones. This is one of the reasons why I believe that there is nothing inherent to monogamy that involves control. It's only in relationships where we actually demand control over our partner's actions and what they do without caring about what they want where I believe there is an issue of control.

When you're thinking of who loves who the most, whether or not your loved one is being loved, or how to even quantify the question, instead remember that all of these are ultimately outside of anyone's control. However, the support you can provide your loved one is absolutely something you can control. Your polyamorous loved one will be able to navigate their relationships if they feel they are not getting the things they need and they can do so even better with your support and love.

7. IS THIS EVEN A REAL RELATIONSHIP?

There are probably nicer ways of asking this question, but sometimes I do think that the emotions of the situation can make loved ones ask things in ways that can be hurtful for their polyamorous loved ones to hear. The concern behind this question I think is around the fear that your loved one might end up getting hurt. Even though it's less about conceptualizing a polyamorous relationship as not as good as a monogamous relationship, that still may be how it feels to your loved one.

It makes sense that you would be concerned about what might happen to your polyamorous loved one. While our way of doing romantic monogamy is fairly new within the spectrum of human experience, it *feels* like something that has been traditional and ongoing for centuries. It is likely that this is the first time you have ever heard of polyamory or anything like it, and monogamy has been the standard by which you and everyone you know has had relationships. Relationships have not been strictly monogamous in some respect throughout time, but everything you've learned or seen about romantic relationships up until this point has been presented to you in a specific way.

It is not surprising, then, that you may worry about the 'realness' of your polyamorous loved one's relationships, the longevity of those relationships, or whether or not it's going to hurt your loved one to be part of them. There is a layer of truth purely in the idea that more relationships will increase the likelihood of more heartbreak, but I'd like to use this section to challenge the assumptions behind this question.

Outline of Relationship

We have a general cultural script around what relationships look like and how they 'progress' that is so culturally reinforced that it feels 'natural' to many of us. Not only does this cultural script define the progression of our romantic relationships, it also defines the digression of other relationships in comparison. It's not uncommon for people to spend a lot of time with their friends and then suddenly spend less time with friends when they have a new romantic partner.

This often feels so 'natural' that people rarely question it, even when it's not a progression that fits them personally. More people today, depending especially on where they live and the culture around them, are starting to peel back the feasibility of this script for every single monogamous person. We're told that a romantic relationship is defined by romantic and sexual exclusivity and time spent together, and that it needs to progress towards cohabitation, marriage, combining or purchasing shared assets, and sometimes having children.

This is the backbone of the way we define what a relationship itself is. One of the things that confuses people the most about polyamory is how, if relationships are defined by exclusivity, a relationship can be 'special' if you share sexual and romantic experiences with others. It's very difficult for people to understand and wrap their heads around the concept that they can have multiple romantic relationships because of this cultural script. And some polyamorous people practise exclusivity in the sense that they may only do one specific activity with one partner to define a progression in their relationship or differentiate one relationship from another.

Truthfully, I think the only way that I can really explain this is that there is a uniqueness in every relationship that doesn't require romantic or sexual exclusivity, in the same way that you can do the exact same activity with multiple friends without detracting from that activity or the friendships, and in the same way that you can do the exact same activity with different children or family members without somehow detracting from that activity or those relationships.

While this is true, legally you can only marry one individual, not everyone wants to move in and cohabitate, and many financial organizations place limits on how many names can be added to bank accounts, credit/debit cards and other structures. But there are monogamous people who have no desire to have children, to cohabitate or to marry, and there are some people who are wilfully and intentionally celibate.

While the inclination is to believe that a relationship is only 'real' if it ticks off the particular milestones that you're used to, there are a lot of people who could benefit from questioning the assumption that one needs to tick off these milestones for the relationship to be 'real'. There might be ways that you could benefit from picking apart this concept for your own relationships.

Different Lifestyles

Another good reason to question the relationship script we have from society is because it quite often isn't a mould that monogamous people want to fit in. The concept that a 'real' relationship hits certain cultural milestones – and that one has to hit these milestones to be happy – has the potential to harm not just your polyamorous loved one but also people who have many, many reasons to not want to hit these milestones.

In a pretty popular interview with *The New York Times* (Hughes, 2022), celebrity Whoopi Goldberg, after being married three times in her life, expressed that she had no interest in remarrying or cohabitating with anybody, famously saying, 'I don't want somebody in my house.' Helena Bonham Carter, who was with director Tim Burton for 13 years, lived in a separate but adjoining property to her partner for many reasons, including Burton's snoring. Bonham Carter told the *Daily Mail* in 2010 that living separately helped strengthen their relationship, noting, 'It's not enforced intimacy. It's chosen, which is quite flattering – if you can afford it' (Thomas, 2010, para. 7). Though they are no longer together, they are not the only famous couple to go against this cultural script.

Our cultural script also truly depends on the society that we live in, even within the US. I remember distinctly the small-talk topic that people brought up most frequently when I lived in rural North Carolina at the age of 22 was whether or not I was married, whereas no one ever asked me that when I lived in California or, later, in London, regardless of my age. I was also frequently asked what church I went to. Now, living in Sweden, marriage is not so common, and most people don't need to get married to their partner in order to gain the benefits that marriage usually brings elsewhere (Meyer, 2021). The cultural expectation of marriage varies wildly.

Today we're becoming more open to the idea that not every single person who gets married is interested in having children, and we don't assume people have to have children in their life in order to be happy in the way we did in previous generations. In 2021, a Pew Research Study found that the rate of non-parents between the ages of 18 and 49 who say they don't want to have children is continuing to grow, and fertility rates in the US were on a general downward trend (Brown, 2021). Deciding not to have children for a variety of reasons, ranging from climate change to financial reasons and medical reasons, is growing.

We're also witnessing a rise of voluntary celibacy in the US and in many countries in Europe, unrelated to religious practices. This is slightly different to 'involuntary celibacy' which is a bit too complicated for me to get into here. But many people are choosing intentionally to not have sexual partners or partners of any kind for all sorts of reasons; it's a trend among Gen Z women which has gained notoriety in press outlets like *The Guardian* (Saner, 2023) and *Cosmopolitan* (Shearing, 2024) leading to a rise in terms like 'boy sober' and the 4B movement in South Korea.

It's becoming clear that the standard narrative to what a 'real' relationship is and what gives us joy and happiness in life is being questioned and shifting. It stands to reason that we might reconsider some of the concepts we've always been taught should accompany a 'relationship' and expand our minds to the different ways we can not only define relationships but seek our own happiness.

Assumptions About Longevity

The big fear behind this question is the worry that, obviously, that which is not 'real' is likely to fade; that a relationship that is not established is not 'real', and can easily be broken. It is very understandable and indeed very human to want to avoid pain and disappointment. While the world is filled with diverse experiences and perspectives, it's a fair thing to say that the vast majority of us do not want to get our hearts broken.

However, there is only so much you can do to avoid pain and heartache. In a famous memoir first published in 2011, *The Top Five Regrets of the Dying*, palliative care nurse Bronnie Ware wrote, after years of caring for the dying, that people's top five regrets were:

1. Not having the courage to live a life true to yourself.
2. Working too hard.
3. Not expressing your feelings.
4. Not staying in touch with friends.
5. Not letting yourself be happier.

While I can't tell you the inner machinations of the minds of every single person that Ware came into contact with, when I look at this list I think that most of the decisions behind them were made out of fear of being hurt or being vulnerable.

We have a better awareness now that breaking up and divorce aren't necessarily failures, even if it feels like this emotionally. No-fault divorce was officially introduced in the US in 1969 in California, so it wasn't that long ago that the idea that divorce was against the public good actually changed. We understand now that it is far better for people to break up than to remain together if they are genuinely unhappy or don't want to stay together.

Of course heartbreak is something that most people wish to avoid and don't want to intentionally cause, but I would encourage you to challenge the assumption that what we consider 'established' and 'real' relationships don't ever lead to heartbreak or that relationships that are 'real' are somehow less likely to end and thus cause heartbreak.

Complexity of Heartbreak

Avoiding heartbreak makes sense, but relationships are far more complex than that. There is an understandable desire to avoid pain and heartbreak in life. Gabor Maté, a physician and expert on addiction, wrote in his book *In The Realm of Hungry Ghosts*:

> At the core of every addiction is an emptiness based in abject fear. The addict dreads and abhors the present moment; she bends feverishly only toward the next time, the moment when her brain, infused with her drug of choice, will briefly experience itself as liberated from the burden of the past and the fear of the future – the two elements that make the present intolerable. (Maté, 2010, p. 262)

A key component of addiction is pain and the avoidance of pain, and not wanting to experience this pain is extremely human. However, I do believe that at times we can become so fearful of the possibility of pain that we create our own pain and suffering through avoidance.

Heartbreak happens no matter what style of relationship you choose. There is only so much one can avoid heartbreak and disappointment in life. The only solution to avoiding all heartbreak in your life would be to forbid yourself from developing any attachments and avoid ever putting yourself out there. As much as I understand the desire to protect a loved one from potential pain, there is such a thing as being so protective that we prevent our loved ones from critical experiences that make up part of their overall story.

There is also a false dichotomy in the understanding that there exist only two types of relationship endings: one where it ends terribly and we are filled with regret and one where we are extremely happy and live out the rest of our days in eternal bliss. But the reality is that life is far, far more complicated than that. Relationships are far more complicated than that. It's not only that the relationships that don't go well have a lot to teach us but also that the upside of many relationships, even if they end in heartbreak, can make the entire experience worth it.

It's absolutely a good instinct to want to protect your loved one from pain and to be concerned that polyamory may lead them towards more pain. I can't tell you that definitely won't be the case, especially since the more relationships you have in your life, statistically there is a higher chance of more frequent heartbreak. But what I can tell you is that things are a lot more complicated than it seems and the one thing that you can definitely provide for your loved one is your support. One thing I can say for sure from my own experience is that of all the heartbreak I have been through, the heartbreak from losing family has been way more difficult to cope with than that of any romance I have had.

8. WHAT ABOUT THEIR FUTURE?

As a parent, it is both understandable and expected to be concerned about the future of your children, other family members, and friends who are like family. Worrying about a loved one's future is generally speaking what well-meaning, loving people do. I say that to highlight that I think that anyone who is generally worried about the future of their polyamorous loved one has their heart in the right place.

What a lot of loved ones don't recognize is that the fear that a polyamorous relationship has less of a 'future' than a monogamous one can stem from the idea that polyamory is not as secure or stable as monogamy. While I do understand why a loved one can think that, especially since the concept of polyamory may be completely new to them, it also makes sense that a polyamorous person may feel upset by the general nature of the question.

Monogamy and Stability

The cultural script of monogamy that we have from society has been told to us since we were small children and for many, many generations. We have a tendency as humans to feel comforted by the thought that an idea is old and therefore tested and reliable. As I was growing up and involving myself in fierce debates for marriage equality, quite often the argument against same-sex marriage was the supposed lack of seriousness of queer love.

I'm grateful that as a society we have surpassed the concept that queer relationships are unstable, but I remember very clearly pictures of very old gay couples who had been together for decades used as evidence of the validity of queer relationships in general. If you are older than I am, you probably also remember this or have seen one or two of these photos. While I hold no grudges against anyone who makes this argument, because it is a decent argument and very true, it does reinforce the idea that long-term monogamous relationships are the best and most stable relationships.

If you asked a random person on the street about marriage and how long we as a society have practised marriage in the way that we practise it today, most people would assume that marriage has been the same since time immemorial, but the truth is that our concept of marriage has radically changed over time. According to the National Women's History Museum (2017), it wasn't until the 18th century that people were actively encouraged to choose marital partners based on romance.

In earlier times, philosophers such as Cicero and Lucretius saw romantic love as a type of illness they actively criticized (Caston, 2006). The word 'platonic' comes from Plato, who believed that non-sexual, brotherly love was the most virtuous form of love. As Dan McClellan, a scholar of the Bible and religion, frequently remarks, the normative social mores that influenced the authors of the Bible, at a time when polygamy was endorsed and normal, saw a romantic sex life as atypical; sex was seen in terms of power as something an active agent does to an object whose consent was largely irrelevant (McClellan, 2024).

Though we perceive marriage for love being a timeless, classic thing, monogamous marriage for love is actually a fairly new concept. My hope in saying that is not that you see monogamous marriage as *less* stable, but that it shifts your perspective into understanding that newer ideas are not necessarily less stable ones. And that older ideas are not necessarily *better* ones for ourselves or for society.

We have a tendency to be afraid of new ideas or new things. As someone who is both polyamorous and non-binary, I have faced a lot of issues with people believing that aspects of my identity are somehow less genuine because they are new words that people have never heard before, even if the concepts behind them are actually pretty old. I don't mind the idea that I've got a new identity though, because I think that which is old is not necessarily better or more traditional.

Challenge yourself a little on the assumption that monogamy is more stable and reliable as a path for your loved one to choose. A lot of the things that seem tried and true are actually fairly new within the continuum of human history. Just because something is newer doesn't mean that it's a less safe path for your loved one.

The Promise of the Future

It's reasonable to want your loved one to live a long, healthy and successful life, but there are all sorts of things that can disrupt the picture we have of a perfect future for someone that we care about. This can happen early in life when parents are faced with the reality that their child might have a condition that will require constant or frequent medical care, for example. Or it can happen because of an accident, a sudden realization that what you thought you wanted was making you deeply unhappy, or even a new burst of passion that pulls us into something we didn't expect.

There are all sorts of identities and situations in life where loved ones have to reconcile themselves with the fact that the future they were told was the best future for their loved one is not the future that lies ahead for them. Part of this, as I have said previously, comes from a place of wanting the best for our loved ones, but another part comes from a reasonable and understandable fear of both pain and death.

Now, I know what you're thinking. Death seems like a heavy subject to bring into a book about relationship styles and love. But death is something I believe we tiptoe around just as much as we have around sexuality, which brings us no real benefit. We will all not only eventually die but also experience the death of many of the people and animals we care about. It is something we fear so much that we avoid the topic and I would like you, for the sake of your loved one and to understand them better, to look at death head on.

Because what lies at the basis of this fear that your loved one is not going to get the stable and secure future that you hoped for is the lingering fear of death. We are comforted by the idea that we're heading down a familiar path because at the end of that familiar path, death sits at a comfortable place which is far away from us. When we go off that path, it reminds us of where it is inevitably directed. Limiting the amount of pain we feel throughout life is incredibly important to many people because of the finite nature of life. Love is infinite, but life is not.

The unfortunate truth of the matter is that whatever future we have planned out or want for our loved one is never guaranteed for anyone. When we go off of the path, I think there is a reminder that the story that is told to us about the life that we should have is not necessarily the story that is guaranteed for any of us. This doesn't mean that there is no point in you imagining a positive future for your loved one or wanting a good life for them, but that any sense of fear or loss you have when the future of your loved one turns out to be different than you imagined is something you can reframe.

Rethink your assumptions of what future you mentally pictured for your loved one and try to remember that there are lots of different futures that your loved one could potentially have, and just because they're not the future that you have been told is the best future doesn't mean that they're not as good: they may even be better.

Future of Loneliness

Having read through some of the relationship styles earlier in this book, you're now more aware of the different ways your loved one might be pursuing polyamory. Different relationship styles may have a different type of future trajectory. If you have a loved one who is interested in a typical hierarchy, then they may be seeking a similar future to the one you have imagined in the past. They may be looking to move in with a partner, combine finances, have children or purchase a house, so you may not have to adjust the future you imagined for them too much.

However, if your loved one is looking more for a solo polyamorous type of life, then their future may look a little different than you imagined. They may not be interested in cohabitating with a loved one or combining finances, but this doesn't necessarily mean that they will spend the rest of their lives lonely and unhappy. In fact, being monogamous in and of itself isn't a guarantee one will end up in a relationship that makes them happy or that will last until the end of their lives. And our picture of a perfect monogamous long-term marriage with a partner isn't necessarily reflected in overall statistics.

According to the American Time Use Survey collected and analysed between 2011 and 2020, the time we spend alone tends to stay pretty constant through our lives, but increases from the age of 55, when we have fewer interactions with colleagues but slightly more interactions with friends (Yau, n.d.). The social script that pins monogamy as the only viable way to live also encourages us to focus on our partner as our primary source of comfort and support, which may actually cause a lot more difficulty for people as they age.

The likelihood of losing a partner as you age depends on a few factors. According to the US Census, in 2016, among those 75 years or older who had ever married, 58 per cent of women and 28 of men had experienced the death of a spouse in their lifetime (Gurrentz & Mayol-Garcia, 2021). The phenomenon of an increased likelihood of a recently widowed person dying is one of the most well documented examples of social relationships on health; one of largest cohort studies conducted in the US of over 373,000 couples indicated that there is a connection between the death of a spouse and the increased likelihood of mortality across multiple causes of death (Elwert & Christakis, 2008). For many older monogamous people, there is a harsh reality in losing a spouse.

This isn't to say that monogamy is a bad choice and we currently do not have any statistics on the specific issues that polyamorous elders face or how common they are compared to what monogamous elders face, but in many cases polyamory can expand the social circle of your loved one, which will provide them with support that they may not typically get within the monogamous social script that many are encouraged to follow. Even for a loved one who practises solo polyamory, the future may still be filled with a lot more love and attention than they might have had otherwise.

Before assuming what your loved one's future will look like, ask them what life they're interested in building with other people. People don't have to live together to have a future together. As much as we're used to this one script for happiness, longevity and an enjoyable life, there are a lot more ways to create a happy life than just this one way we've been told.

Relational Pain and Difficulty

As previously mentioned, pain is a second concern lying behind the worry that people have for their loved ones. They believe that choosing polyamory is a path towards more pain and reasonably want to protect their loved one from that. Some part of this fear is based on a very logical conclusion. The more relationships you have in your life, the higher likelihood some of these relationships might end and therefore the more pain your loved one might experience. So it isn't necessarily out of line to be worried that this path may lead to more pain.

This is a pretty simplistic way of looking at relationships, however. There are a lot of different ways that relationships cause pain. Most of us today are challenging the social scripts that come along with monogamy and it's probably not surprising that many of us no longer believe that staying in a marriage for the rest of your life, even if you are miserable, is always the right solution. But not too long ago, the social consequences of divorce in many societies was too great to consider, even in outwardly abusive relationships.

Still, many express concerns over high divorce rates, trends in celibacy among women, or the way the nature of online dating creates 'too much choice' for many. There is still this underlying fear of people not entering into long-term relationships or leaving those relationships too frequently. While it's understandable that the pain of a breakup may make us feel like ending a relationship is a 'failure', there is no guarantee that a long-term relationship will be happy or provide someone with something that they could not find in other relationships.

While we don't have much data about polyamorous relationships over time, my general observation of polyamorous people is that when one goes against the cultural script provided by monogamy, they are less likely to also stay in relationships that don't serve them. While this isn't always true, because people come to polyamory with their own perceptions of failure when it comes to breakups that encourage them to stay in a relationship (or even open it) to avoid breaking up, I do feel that on the whole, people are a little less inclined and have less social pressure from friends to stay with someone.

Someone who is more likely to stick up for themselves and their wants is more likely to find a relationship that actually meets their needs than someone who goes along with any type of relationship because of social or communal pressure. While there could potentially be more ups and downs for your loved one in their life than they might have had if they had married monogamously and lived in that relationship for the rest of their life, that isn't to say their life is more painful or less filled with joy and happiness.

Challenge the assumption that your loved one is inherently going to face more pain in polyamory than they would in monogamy. If your loved one already has partners, ask them what they enjoy the most about polyamory and what makes them the most happy, and that might make you feel a little less worried about pain.

9. WHAT ABOUT THE CHILDREN?

This is a rough question to be asked if you are a polyamorous parent or want to be one. For this section, I am going to assume that your loved one has children or has expressed a desire to have children. If you're a person who expected your loved one to have or want children, even if they expressed a clear desire not to, that is a larger issue that this book cannot address. I doubt if your loved one gave you this book that you are intent on ignoring what they want in life.

Assuming they do want to have children or already have children, the idea that your polyamorous loved one does not have the best interests of children at heart can be quite difficult for them to hear. But this may not be the intention hidden behind this question. As I've said previously, we have a cultural script of monogamy that has been something that you as a loved one have also been socialized into. Unless you have contradicted this script in some way, you have likely followed a path through life that was meant to lead you and your loved one to happiness.

A big part of this is establishing and raising a family. Growing up in the 1990s with a gay relative, I got to hear a lot about what made a 'stable' family, and even though children don't have to be part and parcel of a marriage, the subject of child rearing always became one of the ways that people would argue that gay people didn't 'need' marriage, as they wouldn't be procreating. The idea of how a family should be structured and what it takes to raise children (specifically, two parents) is something that we all have received strong cultural messages about.

Being concerned about how polyamory might impact children isn't always based on what you believe about polyamory. Especially if you have never heard of polyamory before but have heard all of the other cultural messages, you may not know enough about it to have any informed opinions about it. Here, I will break down some of the assumptions behind this question.

What Children Need

While I am not a parent myself, I have seen enough online content and enough interactions friends have had online to know that often parents really can't win. There are a plethora of different opinions about the way children should be raised that tend to trigger an intense amount of debate. Whether it's how you feed your children, or if you give them specific medications – pretty much anything you do is going to be judged by others in some way.

The subject of children tends to have a way of polarizing people and at times it's for good reasons. Being concerned about the welfare of children isn't a negative thing, but we have to keep in mind that there is a tendency for people to shift towards the side of alarmism and hyper-emotional sensitivity in ways that are sometimes unhelpful and get beyond the actual concern – the welfare of the children.

While there are varying perspectives of the basics of what children need, from a psychological perspective and from basic psychological research published in *The Journal of Education and Research* in 2013, the four main needs of children are:

- orientation and control
- pleasure gain and distress avoidance
- self-esteem protection
- attachment. (Borg-Laufs, 2013)

To summarize some of these needs, orientation and control are about stability or, as Borg-Laufs explains: 'Children need consistent acting caregivers for living in a comprehensible world, who give enough structure on the one hand and on the other hand let their children take part in decisions regarding their development, not overwhelming and not overprotective' (p. 42).

Polyamory provides the opportunity for children to have consistent, multiple acting caregivers, if that is the structure that the individual chooses to have. While, yes, individuals could very well choose caregivers who are irresponsible and don't provide consistency, this is also true of monogamy. There is nothing inherent in polyamory that means caregivers would be any less present.

Pleasure gain and distress avoidance are fairly straightforward, but Borg-Laufs highlights how children need deferment of pleasure and learn to tolerate temporary displeasure in order to have more rewards in the future. Again, nothing about polyamory makes learning to tolerate the deferment of needs any more difficult, and polyamorous parents are just as capable of teaching this as monogamous parents are.

In terms of the protection of self-esteem, parents need to be a consistent source of support for children, as Borg-Laufs confirms: 'Children need to experience success and appreciative feedback from their significant others to satisfy their need for self-protection. Constant criticism, devaluation and abuse by parents undermine the satisfaction of this basic need' (p. 42). Again, there is nothing inherent to polyamory which would mean this need could not be satisfied by parents who are polyamorous, nor anything that monogamous parents could inherently do better by virtue of being monogamous.

Last but not least, attachment is critical because, as Borg-Laufs confirms, attachment between children and their caregivers has an enormous impact on adolescence and, 'A secure attachment style develops through the experience of emotional availability of caregivers in stressful situations' (p. 44). I absolutely do think that parents in polyamorous relationships do need to make sure that the individuals they introduce into their children's lives are capable of providing a secure attachment and a stable environment... but this is also the case for monogamous people.

There is nothing inherent to polyamory that would mean that a child would not get their attachment needs met by their caregivers and, if anything, they might have more caregivers to experience a secure attachment with, rather than fewer. There are more people who could provide childcare and child support. There are more people who could offer a safety net in the exact same way many monogamous parents have extended family members who also provide that support.

Based on what we know about what children need from their caregivers, polyamory in and of itself doesn't hinder meeting a child's basic needs.

Different Family Structures

When we are in panic or concern mode, we sometimes forget the nuances of the world around us and we jump towards black-and-white assumptions. This isn't intentional: in life-or-death situations, our brains evolved to make things black and white to survive. Either something is dangerous or it's not, and in the past we needed to make snap decisions to save our own lives.

So when you ask this question, it's likely that you're forgetting about all of the different types of family structures that exist now and have existed throughout time. The typical two-parent family structure is actually pretty new within the context of our society, as previously discussed in 'Polyamory isn't wrong' in the section '2. Did I do something wrong?' Even today, it is somewhat a privilege to have older relatives and other extended family members who never need to live with you or rely on you for support physically or economically.

Growing up, there were a few instances where my aunts lived with us and took part in providing childcare and there have also been times where family members have supported one another by having relatives live with them. This isn't a practice that's necessarily restricted to individuals of lower incomes. In many cultures it is expected for people to support their parents in their older age.

In 2020, according to the US Census, 7.2 per cent of US households were multi-generational (three or more generations under one roof), an increase from 4.7 per cent in 2010, with multi-generational households being more common in the South, Puerto Rico and some western states and less common in the Northeast and Midwest (Washington et al., 2023). There are likely cultural elements at play but what's important to remember is that our assumptions of what a typical family looks like aren't always accurate, depending on the culture, and as the cost of living increases, we may see further growth of multi-generational families.

A typical, two-parent household is not really required for a successful environment for a child to grow up in. According to the National Scientific Council on the Developing Child (2015), stable and committed relationships with adults in a child's life help buffer them from developmental disruption during hardships and build resilience. It stands to reason that the more positive, supportive relationships a child has in their lives, the better their life will be overall.

While you may be concerned that more partners may mean more instability in the lives of any current or future children your loved one may have, there are two considerations here: not every single partner that your loved one has may be or even want to be involved as a parental figure within the life of a child, and it's fully possible that a monogamous person could have the same amount of instability within their lives as a polyamorous person. Monogamy as a chosen lifestyle is not inherently more stable.

In a study on the impact of family structure on children based on three decades of research (Anderson, 2014), though it focused specifically on the effects of divorce, it was found that divorce overall did have a negative impact on children as a result of one or more of these factors:

- The child got less time with each parent.
- The child lost economic security.
- The child lost emotional security as parents were less able to provide emotional support.
- The child lost access to religious communities.
- The child lost access to adults who could support their educational development.

There are other factors within the study that I think can be attributed to lower economic security or aren't in my opinion necessarily 'problems' (such as changing outlook on sexual behaviour). This isn't to say that adults should stay together if they are miserable, because a longitudinal study conducted on children aged from two to ten (Brock & Kochanska, 2016) also documented that parental conflict has a huge impact on children's psychology in the long term in multiple ways.

The point is that frequent conflict and instability can happen within monogamous relationships. All parents, polyamorous or not, should be aiming to provide their child with stable, reliable, supportive and present adults within their life. It makes sense to be concerned about the impact of multiple adults being introduced to children as important figures in their lives and then suddenly disappearing, but make sure you aren't assuming that your polyamorous loved one will be irresponsible with the environment of their children or future children.

And let's not forget that you have the ability to provide another supportive, caring adult in the life of your loved one's child, and losing that opportunity by creating unnecessary conflict isn't something that will help the child.

Legal Considerations

Depending on where your loved one is located, there may be some legal considerations that you could potentially help out with. While 'polyamory' is a new word and a new type of relationship style that has formed over the years, most people are familiar with polygamy, which is slightly different. Polygamous marriage is legal in many countries, though banned in most of the US. I would argue that polygamous marriage is not really what those polyamorous people who do want marriage would want.

While 'polygamy' is *technically* a gender-neutral term, when it is used today the vast majority of people imagine a situation where a man is allowed to have multiple wives but those wives are not allowed other partners and a woman cannot have multiple husbands. In some places where polygamous marriage is permitted, these are not relationships that allow for equality between all partners or recognize all partners' ability to marry others.

Not only are no forms of polyamorous marriage legally recognized, but in 16 US states, adultery is illegal and considered a crime. This means that if your loved one is legally married, which may be something that polyamorous people do if they have children or need access to health insurance, even just being polyamorous may cause a legal issue. And if it causes a legal issue, it may also cause an issue around the custody and care of children, where a court may consider what is in the best interest of a child.

According to Dr Elisabeth Sheff (2017), it is rare for Child Protective Services in the US to take away a child purely on the grounds of the parents being polyamorous or practising polyamory. However, I think as someone who wants to support your loved one, whether that be monetarily or reaching out to networks that could provide monetary or legal support, making sure that your loved one is as supported as possible could make them feel more secure.

Where polyamorous adults can't have the federal or state institutions of marriage to provide them with protection, it is possible to form legal contracts or utilize adoption systems to provide more legal backing to protect parents and children in different circumstances. While I don't think you need to be excessively worried about the legality of everything going on in your loved one's life, where you can provide support, do offer it.

Naturalness of Monogamy

Another aspect that people often lean upon or are concerned about when it comes to children is a perception that a two-parent monogamous household is more 'natural' and that in and of itself is better for children. While the argument around what is better for children is slightly different from arguing that monogamy is more 'natural', I often find that these two assumptions are pretty linked.

Historically, one of the arguments against same-sex marriages or adoptions, or allowing single queer people to adopt, was that same-sex relationships were not 'natural'. I could see a similar argument frequently being leveraged against polyamorous people with regard to the safety of children.

I could go through the tree of human evolution, point out the behaviours of bonobos, who are more closely related to us than species like gorillas, or the many, many examples throughout nature where monogamy is uncommon or only temporary. I could pretty much reproduce the entirety of Christopher Ryan and Cacilda Jethá's book *Sex at Dawn* (Ryan & Jethá, 2010) here or cite the same research the book uses to underpin the argument that polyamory is just as 'natural' as monogamy is.

But personally, I actually think this isn't that useful an approach. Many people have made the point that arguing that sexual orientation is something you're born with implies that one wouldn't choose to be anything but heterosexual and reinforces that heterosexuality is better. Arguing that polyamory is just as 'natural' as monogamy creates the same sort of issue.

The fact of the matter is that we don't currently live in a fully 'natural' world. It seems ironic for us to be concerned about the 'natural' state of our relationships while also caring less about the natural environment and the circumstances that keep us alive in the natural world. This, of course, depends on what you define as 'natural', but many of the technological advances that we have today that are responsible for extending our lives are not natural.

And not everything that is natural is automatically good or beneficial. In addition to citing all of the examples of non-monogamy throughout the animal kingdom, I could also explore a lot of animal behaviours we would consider to be deeply immoral or messed up that also fall under the category of 'natural'.

If you want to explore the 'naturalness' of non-monogamy, I could recommend reading *Sex at Dawn* for a more extended explanation of that concept and the way that monogamy may have developed in human societies, but overall I would question what 'natural' means and whether or not what is 'natural' is better.

10. IS IT JUST ABOUT SEX?

This is awkward, I'm not going to lie, depending on what type of loved one you are to the polyamorous person who would hope that you read this book. Chances are if you are a relative, it's unlikely that your polyamorous loved one is going to want to discuss the ins and outs of their sex life with you, though some people will have different types of relationships with their loved ones. In many of the situations where I have given advice to folks or seen people concerned about coming out to their families, there has been a concern about whether talking about polyamory will lead to intimate questions about their sex life.

Hopefully this book can bridge the gap between you and your loved one and I can address some of the issues that come up with this question so that they don't have to. While a lot of people can feel judged by this question, I don't think judgement is always the intention, as with most of the questions in this book. Despite how it may come across, I think the concern you have as a loved one is about whether or not your loved one could either be being taken advantage of or not be getting a deep, meaningful relationship.

There are lots of ways that I could challenge these assumptions, not just through the definition of polyamory itself but by questioning the idea of what makes something deep and meaningful. Throughout this section my hope is that I can address this question and avoid an awkward conversation between you and your loved one.

Sex-Negative Society

Inherent within this question is the assumption that a relationship that is based purely on sex is a problem. As an American who has lived in Europe for 15 years, I can tell you that attitudes towards sex, even if polyamory is still relatively rare, vary wildly, and different states in the US may have different perspectives. A lot of people even today still have the belief that a relationship that is 'just sex' is empty or missing something critical or that sexual needs are not real needs within relationships.

The concept that a sexually focused or based relationship is 'less than' is something that you frequently see even within polyamorous communities. If you've already asked this question to your loved one, it's likely that they emphasized the definition of polyamory in that it focuses on building romantic relationships and not 'just sex'. I have frequently found an attitude among many polyamorous people of a type of sex negativity where there is a tacit judgement against people who are looking for 'just sex' and an assumption of what a more casual relationship may consist of.

Polyamory is focused around building multiple romantic relationships that may or may not include sex, but that doesn't necessarily prevent people from forming more casual relationships or relationships that might be described as 'just sex'. Different people can conceptualize their relationships in different ways, but it is wrong to assume that a relationship with less expectation of commitment is less 'deep' or meaningful to the people in them. Many mono-centric societies encourage people to view friendships as less than romantic relationships. Not everyone who is polyamorous is a relationship anarchist and many people do have a hierarchical approach to how they form relationships. However, I would argue that most people actually do highly value their friendships and that experiencing a breakup of a friendship can actually be just as or sometimes more painful and difficult than a romantic breakup. For that reason, we shouldn't assume that a 'friends with benefits' situation *isn't* deep or meaningful for the people involved.

Attitudes towards sex and its importance in relationships begin arguably with sex education, which is inconsistent and inadequately delivered in the US. Despite the fact that the Center for Disease Control (CDC) in the US recommends 20 essential topics to be covered in sex education, a 2018 study cited by the Duke Centre for Global Reproductive Health found that fewer than half of high schools and fewer than one fifth of middle schools touched on those topics (Shah, 2022). Many in the US support the concept of abstinence-only sex education despite overwhelming evidence that it does not work. It's unsurprising then that many people don't feel fully confident about expressing or asking about their sexual needs.

That then carries over and reinforces the idea that relationships that are 'just sex' are less valuable, less important or shallower. I could have started this section by arguing about what the definition of polyamory is, how it's not 'just sex' but it's focusing on building romantic relationships, typically for the long term. However, I would rather not reinforce the idea that relationships that are not long term, that don't involve explicit commitments, or are more similar to friendships than romantic relationships are less important or not valuable. Even if your loved one currently has no romantic relationships designed to be long term or has some friends with benefits, those relationships may still be valuable and important to your loved one.

Challenge any assumption that you may have about what 'just sex' means within a relationship and assume that your loved one wants you to be part of their life but may not necessarily need to talk about the ins and outs of their private life with you. Even if you are curious, I would definitely recommend respecting the boundaries of your loved one around discussing this.

Asexual Polyamorists Exist

Aside from explaining that polyamory is focused on building multiple romantic relationships, it's also important to point out that asexuality is something that does exist and asexual people may be specifically interested in polyamory for a variety of reasons.

Research on sexual orientation identities often doesn't include 'asexual' as a means of identification so we can't always be sure that we have the full information on the commonality of asexuality. Not to mention, there is a significant stigma that asexual people face and people struggle to come to terms with this identity in similar ways to other LGBTQ identities.

According to one study, quantitative research on a population-based sample of lesbian, gay, bisexual and other sexual minority people in the US found that many asexuals (though a small sample size given the number of respondents) face anger, disbelief and pathologizing when telling others about their identity, and many have elevated levels of social withdrawal (Rothblum et al., 2020). This may explain why so many are hesitant to come out as asexual and why asexuality was also only reported in about 1.66 per cent of the population-based sample they collected.

It's worth noting that as much as the term 'asexual' may be understood by most people as 'people who aren't interested in having sex', there are actually complexities within the umbrella of asexuality. According to the Asexual Visibility and Education Network (n.d.), an asexual person is defined specifically as 'someone who does not experience sexual attraction or an intrinsic desire to have sexual relationships'. Within this umbrella are people who:

- never experience any sexual attraction
- do experience *some* sexual attraction but rarely
- experience sexual attraction but only in specific circumstances.

People who are asexual can experience things like romantic attraction but without a sexual element. There is no real way I can fully encapsulate the complexity of how people feel about attraction and romance. In fact, I feel like the more we try to pin everything down in boxes, the *less* successful we will be at really representing our nuance and complexity. What's important to understand here is that people who don't have a normative experience of sexual attraction can have an interest in polyamory.

The reasons for this can vary. Someone who discovers their asexuality later on in life may find themselves in a marriage they don't wish to dissolve and may decide to open their relationship in order to maintain their otherwise happy and functioning partnership. However, it's important to note that polyamory isn't about 'fixing' asexuality. Asexual people may seek out polyamory not to 'fix' anything or address an imbalance but because they desire multiple romantic relationships. Polyamory doesn't 'fix' the problems asexuals may face in an allosexual (or non-asexual) world just as polyamory doesn't 'fix' the obstacles people may face in all aspects of their life.

As a loved one, knowing about this is less about having to fully 'get' your polyamorous loved one's sexuality and more about understanding the idea that not every polyamorous relationship includes sex, so it can't be 'just about sex'.

Definition of Polyamory

The number one argument against the idea that polyamory is 'just about sex' is the definition – polyamory is about the intent to establish multiple romantic relationships. To note, you don't have to currently be dating more than one person or any person at all to identify with polyamory or to be polyamorous. It's less about being in as many relationships as possible and more about the *intent* of how you want to live – just as you don't need to be partnered to be monogamous.

As we've reviewed in the section '2. Words You Might Run Into' in Part 1 of the book, there are a variety of ways people may decide to live polyamorously. They may want to be solo polyamorous and live alone but have other partners they visit, or they may wish to have a relationship that may resemble your own or ones you have been in, in that they desire to have one live-in partner and establish a shared household with a family.

I have addressed in other questions that we often believe

that monogamous romantic relationships in the way they exist today are a lot more traditional than they actually are. It's quite often because of this feeling of the 'traditional' couple that many people find it difficult to wrap their heads around why someone might be interested in polyamory. But, according to the Institute for Family Studies, throughout history and across the vast majority of human societies, we lived in polygamous societies (Carroll, 2021).

However, I deeply and personally believe in contradicting the belief that older practices are inherently better. Human societies have done a lot of things for centuries that were morally bankrupt. Looking back at polygamy practices over time, the vast majority of them look nothing like modern-day polyamory in the approach of actually caring about the consent and autonomy of all of those involved.

I'm not keen on even accidentally supporting systems that I believe were less about love and more about giving powerful people freedom to do what they would like to do without consequence. Nor am I keen to attribute the relative peace many enjoy in modern society purely to the adoption of monogamy. I think things are a bit more complicated than that.

What we can at least learn from humanity's interest in polygamy over time is that there is nothing inherently more 'natural' about single pair bonds, nor anything more inherently 'natural' about multiple pair bonds. While we may feel that monogamy is more 'natural' because it is what our societies practise today, historically we have had very different concepts of the importance of romance and how it plays in our society today.

As a loved one, understanding the very basics of the definition of polyamory and how romance is part of it might help you feel a little more grounded, though I would still encourage you to challenge the initial idea that sexually based relationships are negative.

The Value of Family

If you've read any of the other questions, you understand that the support of loved ones is incredibly critical. I can re-emphasize this point here but I want to ask the obvious question – if this was 'just about sex', would your loved one be that interested in letting you know about that or asking for your support or even giving you the information? This depends on the relationship you have with your loved one, but more likely than not, they don't tend to seek out your affirmation for other things they're interested in that are just about sexuality.

Even within fairly progressive social circles where all types of different ways that people are disenfranchised are explored, I find that there is very little discussion on the importance of proper family support. While I don't think it is clear whether it is more harmful to have a family present in your life than no family at all, I am going to assume that if someone you love has given you this book, you fall into the supportive and present family camp.

A 2019 study published in the journal *Mental Health and Prevention* stated that the social bonds between children and their families are critically important: 'social bonds between children and their parents can be regarded as social capital – including norms and values – which may be as important as financial and human capital for health and well-being' (Grevenstein et al., 2019). Overall, the study found that 'better family relationship quality was linked to better health and well-being, higher life satisfaction, and individual salutogenic characteristics'. Overall, strong family support has a clear benefit to individuals in multiple aspects.

Another study published in 2017 on family relationships and well-being stated the importance of parent–child relationships even as the child becomes an adult, noting that, while it can get complicated if the adult becomes a caregiver to their parent, 'intergenerational support exchanges are integral to the lives of both parents and adult children, both in times of need and in daily life' (Thomas, Liu & Umberson, 2017). Other familial relations are somewhat understudied but the study states that overall 'family relationships provide resources that can help an individual cope with stress, engage in healthier behaviors, and enhance self-esteem, leading to higher well-being'.

Your polyamorous loved one is likely reaching out to you or telling you about this aspect of their life to maintain a relationship with you and to foster a deeper connection going forward. As a loved one, whether you are a parent or not, you have the opportunity to focus less on the details that might be somewhat interesting from a curiosity standpoint and more on providing much-needed support for your loved one.

Facebook introduced the 'open relationship' status in 2011 following the addition of 'It's complicated' in 2005, a year after Facebook itself launched. People are somewhat aware of non-monogamy but often only in a peripheral way. This means that the network of support your loved one has even if they have a large friendship network may be quite small. Where people would typically seek help when confused about a relationship problem, most polyamorous people can't necessarily do so if their social circle is mostly monogamous.

Consider that as a loved one, you can provide critical and needed support to your loved one, and that them telling you that they are polyamorous is not about them inviting you into the details of their sex life, but instead wanting you to know about something that is part of their daily life or identity.

∞

Part 3: Providing Support

1. THE FAMILY SURVEY

In an attempt to better understand the diversity of experience polyamorous people have with their family members, I launched a survey in the summer of 2024 to gather responses from individuals about their personal experiences in coming out to family members. I did my best on social media and through the help of others and received over 120 responses.

I asked the question 'Have you ever felt judged or rejected by a family member for being polyamorous?' and only 29 per cent reported 'No'. With such a low number of people reporting not feeling judged or rejected, I wanted to go beyond these responses and learn more about different perspectives and experiences while also providing you with guidance on what you can do differently.

2. LISTENING WITHOUT JUDGEMENT

Understand that you're on the same team.
Learn how to provide a listening space without
immediately trying to 'solve' things.
Validate feelings and echo sentiments.
Ensure your own needs are met and set
boundaries before you try to help others.

My great grandmother in all of her wisdom used to say, on the subject of going to school and getting decent grades, that if you can't do anything else, you can at least sit down and be quiet. Of course, that is a little harsher than I want to come across here. If you're someone with a polyamorous loved one and you're reading this book, I'm going to assume you want to do more than just hold your tongue about polyamory. For as much as I do believe tolerance is important, acceptance is much more important, especially coming from a loved one.

Accepting your loved one doesn't have to mean that you feel positively about polyamory or even that you think it's a good idea. I truly feel you're welcome to your own beliefs about what would be best for your loved one. But I do think that acceptance means reserving judgement and providing an open space for your loved one to come to, not because you believe in polyamory but because you believe that you're both on the same team and you want the same things.

One of the best ways to pull back from even the most intense conflict I have found is remembering that we're all on the same team. If you're in any kind of relationship, you should both want the best for one another. Setting your personal feelings aside to present a presence of understanding can be a really valuable thing for your loved one. Part of doing this may involve switching up your typical communication style.

I'm very much a problem solver, which is why I have been doing a non-monogamy advice podcast and column for so long. When I see a problem, I immediately want to fix it. I have really had to learn to hold back when someone is telling me about a problem and ask them if they are looking for advice, empathy or both, because I have learned the hard way that not all problems can be solved by me and that it's not my job to solve every problem.

Through therapy I learned that I often assume I have to be useful to be loved, so this desire to solve problems runs deep. Learning that just listening can be more useful has been a good way to 'hack' that instinct, but it does take conscious effort. You may want to 'solve' your loved one's problems if they come to you to talk about the ups and downs of polyamory and see you as a safe space to discuss these issues. Just remember that you don't always have to solve every single problem. Sometimes just listening is the solution.

If you're like me and you want to do more than just sit and listen because you do actually want to make it clear that you're providing support, I've found it really helpful to try and repeat people's feelings back to them in a way that I understand. You know how people say that the best way to understand a concept is to teach it to someone else or explain it to someone else in the simplest way possible? I take that same approach to emotions other people have, especially as someone who struggles sometimes to put myself exactly in their shoes.

So when listening, saying something like, 'It sounds like

you're experiencing X' or 'This sounds really Y'. Echoing your loved one's sentiments and feelings may help them explore them further and also help them feel that they are being listened to rather than you just sitting and nodding. It can also help you understand where they are coming from better, because instead of being focused on the idea of solving their problem, you're solving the 'problem' of understanding where they are coming from and how they are feeling.

Last but not least, it's very important that you manage your own boundaries and ability to listen. I have friendships with people where we discuss our sex lives and details about our bodies but I have other friendships where we never discuss anything like that and where if I did, it might make my friend uncomfortable. I don't *need* to discuss these types of details with those friends to have close, meaningful relationships.

Yes, you want to be supportive of your loved one, but it's also okay for you to have your own boundaries put in place and for you to ask for some space or some time to adjust if that's what you need. Even if you are a parent in the mix of this situation, you are still a human and you still may not be able to be a fountain of endless support and validation for your loved one – and they shouldn't expect you to.

You truly can't pour from an empty cup and you need to secure your mask before you try to help other people. If you need a moment to yourself or if there are things you don't want to discuss, it's okay to ask your loved one for space, or for some privacy around different things. Remember that boundaries are not about punishment. When you put boundaries down around the types of things you can hear from your loved one or the time you have, this should be out of a desire to bring you closer together.

We can't all be endless providers of support and adoration

for everyone we love in our life. Sometimes we really need space for ourselves and truly, if we want to remain close to our loved ones, we have to be responsible for telling them what our needs are, even if it makes us uncomfortable to do so. Sometimes when we avoid telling people what we genuinely need, we end up actually pushing ourselves further away from them because betraying ourselves by doing things we don't want to do often creates resentment over time.

Now, of course, relationships often have give and take. People who care about us sometimes get on our nerves and I'm not saying that you should only ever do things that you want to do and that sacrifice isn't part of a good relationship. But make sure you're balancing your own needs with the needs of your loved one in a way that leaves you feeling empowered or closer rather than used and distant.

Personal Story: Peter

After a bit of research, Peter and his wife assumed that both of their families might begin from a place of judgement and pessimism but that over time, they would become more open to it. However, his experience has actually been the opposite.

Initially Peter was researching possibilities to repair the connection between himself and his wife after experiences of infidelity. After getting the support of a therapist, they decided to open up, though Peter still felt monogamous. After branching out and trying dating, Peter discovered that polyamory actually fit him pretty well. 'As a teenager, I remember having multiple crushes on people simultaneously. As I kept learning more about polyamory, it made more and more sense as a part of my identity and as a relationship structure that works best for me.' Once both he and his wife were confident that polyamory wasn't just something they did, but part of who they were, not telling family morphed from being about privacy to secrecy, and it became more and more difficult to hide these aspects of themselves.

One Easter family weekend, they both decided to take the plunge and tell both of their families during their visit. For Peter, the actual conversation went well but over time, discussions became more and more judgemental. Culturally, Peter's parents could be extremely direct and had few filters. This helped conversations move forward and become open but over time, as more and more judgements came through, so did the hurt which led to Peter's wife setting some boundaries to take some time away from seeing Peter's parents, which impacted Peter's relationships with both his spouse and his family. 'I wish I had set clearer boundaries to prevent my parents from saying so many judgemental and hurtful things to my wife and me.' Before, he would see family several times a year and a chat on the phone once per week, but because of the distance, the talks have become less frequent.

The conversations Peter had with family felt circular and always ended up being the same conversation, without much learning or progress. While they may have been open to resources and more information in the beginning, Peter isn't sure now how open they might continue to be and hopes other polyamorous people can learn from this surprising trajectory. 'Polyamorous people who come out may need to learn into periods of time in which their loved ones are open to learning how they can best support them because those periods of time, like in our case, may not be long-lasting.'

Personal Story: Luna

Though appearing on the outside to be idyllic, Luna's connection to her traditional, wealthy parents was strained, especially after a non-mutual and emotionally difficult divorce that caused a large split within her family. Sitting in the middle of family members who didn't get along created more than one obstacle for her when it came to thinking about who and how to discuss polyamory with.

Her own personal curiosity about sexuality as well as the crack in her parent's foundational monogamy made Luna curious to explore other options. After travelling and meeting others who were non-monogamous, the possibility opened up for her to have two travelling partners who knew about each other, which made her realize that polyamory was a real possibility. Luna had different relationships, some long and some short, but mostly Luna kept polyamory to herself, so her parents assumed her relationships were monogamous. There were a lot of reasons for avoiding the discussion with her parents, including not really wanting to hear their advice about her romantic life, not wanting to be thought of as 'broken' and needing fixing, and protecting her partner, an immigrant to her country, from judgement. 'They had been quite passive-aggressive towards him about his integration journey, his language skills, and his work ethic. I didn't want to add another aspect of a thing where they would judge him more.'

After the relationship between herself and this partner ended, different pieces of the truth began spilling out from the cracks when her mother began asking about different situations, and hiding the truth became more difficult. Finally after being asked about a 'new man' in her life, Luna sat her parents down and had a conversation about non-monogamy and how she wanted to go forward. At first, there weren't many questions, but then after a while, many of her parents' fears and worries came through – worries about what would happen if Luna got sick and the assumption that it was the big, acrimonious divorce that 'caused' her to be interested in non-monogamy. 'Their projections of her fears on my life were very harsh for me. I left the room several times to regulate instead of blowing up in her face because I was so angry.'

The initial discussion has since calmed down, but Luna has yet to come out to any other family members, except for a sibling who took it in their stride. She wants to continue to protect any future partners from harsh judgement because she doubts that they would be seen as 'ideal partners' for her. Before coming out to her parents, they were always interested in Luna's romantic life, but that interest has waned and Luna is also less interested in bringing up the subject. The experience of coming out to her parents has made her significantly hesitant to come out to other family members, and she is focusing on trying to figure out why she needs to do so, rather than how.

'I wish my parents would be more capable of distinguishing their own fears from what is important in my life and ask questions in a respectful, calm way. I wish they could have regulated their emotions before dumping them onto me.' Though the situation has caused Luna a lot of frustration, she acknowledges that the lack of media, literature or documentaries accessible for her parents has likely had an impact on their understanding of non-monogamy and that, if things had been different, she might have had a different coming out experience.

3. SHOWING INITIATIVE AND INTEREST

Be curious about your loved one's internal experience.
Demonstrate the basics of your knowledge.
Ask if they have the space to explain things.
It's okay if you don't understand things.

After providing a listening and supportive environment without judgement, the next step up you can do to be supportive is to show some initiative and interest in your loved one's life. You can still of course maintain your boundaries around details or times when you're unavailable to provide support, but being curious about their internal experience is a great way to start.

Almost everyone who is polyamorous has some type of story to tell about how they figured out they were polyamorous or what got them interested in polyamory. It may be something they have always felt or it might be something that slowly came up through a variety of experiences. If you don't want to get into the details of sexuality, you can always ask for the safe-for-work version of the story, but being curious about the journey that your loved one has gone on is a great way to show interest in their life.

You can also ask them about the community that's around them. Polyamory communities can vary wildly and I always refer to them with the UK expression of 'postcode lottery' where it's pure luck whether the community around you can be really great or really bad. Either way, it's a topic of discussion and it's something that your loved one may have explored and have a lot to talk about.

Additionally, you can ask if they have any new crushes or new interests. I had a friend who would always ask me whenever we caught up if I'd been on any new dates and even though I am someone who doesn't feel much attraction to many people, it was really nice to see that she had an interest in my life and what was going on, and was excited for me. Showing some enthusiasm for your loved one's ability to have new experiences is another way to be supportive.

Don't get me wrong, the dating scene can be really rough as a polyamorous person. Contrary to what many people might assume, being polyamorous does in fact *shrink* your dating circle rather than expand it. We often don't have a very wide circle of available people so you might also hear your loved one complain about the state of dating instead of hearing about new loves or crushes – but that also has its place in terms of providing support.

In reading this book, you've done some basic work to learn more about polyamory. Even if you're not interested in being polyamorous, at the end of the book I include some suggested further reading that you could explore if you wanted to learn more about being polyamorous. Still, demonstrating knowledge by using the correct terms for things (such as 'metamour' or 'new relationship energy' (NRE)) can sometimes be a really heartening sign that someone is trying to understand you and show that they understand.

Of course, everyone is different and I can't promise this will be meaningful for all polyamorous people, but demonstrating your knowledge where you can is something that can go far with a lot of people and help them understand that you're doing the work on your own to learn more about polyamory rather than them having to explain everything.

Sometimes polyamorous people can feel isolated because they can't just speak to people plainly about what's going on in their relationships without having to explain everything. Showing that you understand some of the basics can not only help your loved one feel a little less alone but also help them come a little bit more out of their shell and understand that they can rely on you if they need someone to talk to.

Personal Story: Dean

Growing up with a bisexual mother, Andrea, who was extremely supportive, Dean didn't have much fear around telling his parents about being polyamorous, having always felt close to both his mother and his sibling. During his teenage years, two of Dean's friends asked if they could all be together as a triad, which was his first introduction to anything resembling polyamory. Though that was a long time ago, he still remained friends with them.

Almost immediately, Dean shared the information with his mother. 'I knew there wasn't going to be any judgement,' he said. This supportive atmosphere has made many experiences of being on the outside, including being transgender, much easier for Dean to manage. When it comes to experiences with extended family, Dean's mother Andrea has even stepped up to help work with other members of the family to understand better.

Though there has been some disconnect through divorce

and a lack of extended family, Andrea has taken the lead in speaking to her own siblings in casual conversations. The topic of speaking to his grandmother about not only Dean's gender identity but also polyamory has made him a little nervous: 'I'm really nervous to tell her in person because you never know someone's reaction.'

There is a further complication with Dean's grandmother because she may be experiencing memory issues. Andrea has stepped up to offer to have the discussions needed with her mother first over the phone so Dean has a safer experience and still have some time with her while he can have it.

Andrea has stepped in to follow polyamory content creators and is always highly receptive to anything that Dean sends over about polyamory.

Personal Story: Vivian

Vivian had grown up without being pressured actively into any specific lifestyles, but the gap between her own understanding of sexuality and identity and her parents' was difficult to jump across. While they wouldn't condemn someone for their identity, taking it seriously was another thing. When another sibling had his own coming-out journey with their parents, a lot of the basic questions about sexuality were answered, but Vivian still experienced a lot of doubt about her parents' sincerity when she learned about asexuality and demisexuality at school. Not being on the same page as her parents and having to re-explain things was difficult, but she was still grateful for the effort her parents were putting in.

'I'm so glad I have parents who are willing to learn. They have come a long way.'

By the time polyamory became something she wanted to be honest about, Vivian was living as an adult with a family dynamic that changed after her parents' divorce. She and her partner were living in and paying rent for her mother's downstairs studio due to a COVID lockdown. 'I definitely wouldn't have told them, but my metamour was coming to visit my partner and me.' After witnessing her sibling's own coming out, she did have a desire to open up more to her parents but the sudden visit catapulted the moment into now and forced her to confront conversations she had avoided for a long time. Her dad expressed concern for her being taken advantage of but ultimately felt that if Vivian was happy, that was fine. But with her mom, things were a lot different. The end result was anger on both sides, frustration and a bit of distance that was eventually healed. Now Vivian admits that she could have had the conversation earlier and she wishes it hadn't been so explosive. 'I just wish there was no "coming out". I want a point in time where I can tell them I have partners. I wish I could be excited and they would be excited for me.'

Now it is a continuous conversation that has got better, but some questions still keep getting repeated. Being less closed off from her parents has brought Vivian closer to them, but Vivian admits that it can be exhausting to educate people and defend herself against strange, even well-meaning assumptions. The added pressure of feeling under the judgement of others can feel overwhelming at times. 'I feel a sense of responsibility for my relationships to be perfect and to prove that polyamory can and does work. Monogamous people don't have to do that.'

Vivian isn't sure how much her extended family knows, but she continues to hope that her parents talk about it normally if it ever comes up. 'I don't want to keep having the same conversations about it again and again.' Despite the challenges, she is optimistic that things will continue to improve over time.

4. MEETING OTHER PARTNERS

Offering to meet your loved one's partners
is a great way to extend your support.
It's okay to be awkward – let yourself be awkward!
Talk with your loved one about hierarchy
and what it means for them.
If you don't know – just ask!

In many of the questions and scenarios I've introduced above, I've mentioned that loved ones have a particularly significant role to play in the lives of polyamorous people just as they would monogamous people in terms of meeting partners. Most people would understand why meeting their loved one's partner would be really important within a monogamous context but may feel extremely hesitant to meet more than one partner.

First, I want to say that any anxiety that you may feel in meeting your loved one's other partners is totally and completely normal and doesn't necessarily reflect your acceptance or lack thereof of polyamory. We have to remember, as I've mentioned before, that there are social scripts with monogamy that we have had playing in the background all of our lives that don't exist for polyamory. Because of that, there are a lot of situations that will be completely new for you.

It makes sense and is a completely human response to be nervous and afraid in new situations or around things that you have no social script for. The nervousness and fear are not necessarily something you can control, but what you decide to do with that fear is within your control. Many people respond to fear with distrust and rejection. I assume if you are reading this book, you do not want to distrust or reject your loved one. But understanding that your emotions make rational sense and don't reflect some sort of inner desire to reject your loved one is an important step.

Offering to meet other partners can go a long way in terms of how supported your loved one feels. It's one thing to sit and listen and nod your head, but meeting other partners and demonstrating your ability to put effort into getting to know more about your loved one's life can go a long way. Depending on the type of polyamory your loved one is practising, you may only meet one partner, you may meet multiple partners or you may not meet any at all – it truly depends! If you're curious about offering to meet other partners, you can talk to your loved one directly.

If you do have active plans to meet partners, a big thing that I would encourage you to do is, instead of trying to prevent yourself from feeling awkward, instead *embrace* the awkwardness. One of the things I encourage polyamorous people to remember when they are meeting their metamours – or their partner's partners – is that it may be a little bit awkward or very awkward *and that is okay*. What can make these situations a little more difficult is when we put pressure on ourselves to feel or be a certain way.

It's quite often that our expectations of the way a situation should go end up creating an idealized version of ourselves so that we feel like a failure if we don't measure up to it. In this way we can become the architects of our own misery because the only person with that expectation of ourselves is often... ourselves! Obviously your loved one wants you to be kind and courteous, but beyond just trying to be nice, there is nothing inherently rude or bad about being a little bit awkward.

As someone who is neurodivergent, I struggle with understanding how other people feel about me at any given moment. For reference, a neurodivergent person is someone whose mental or neurological systems operate differently than most people and is often used to describe people on the autistic spectrum, with attention deficit hyperactivity disorder (ADHD) and other conditions that affect how they process information. I worry pretty exponentially about being 'rude' or being seen as rude. I can absolutely understand being afraid to step on toes or say something that lands your foot squarely in your mouth. I try my best to make sure people understand, especially those I truly care about, that if I ever sound harsh or personal, I likely don't mean to be.

For a while now, I have had to let go of the idea that I could control the version of me that other people have in their heads. Obviously, if I have hurt someone, I do my best to apologize if they make me aware of it. But I can only do that if they make me aware of it. And I can't really help it very much if someone met me on the wrong day, maybe I was a bit brusque with them, and they walked away from that exchange believing me to be a truly horrible person.

Understandably, we don't want the people we love and care about to think we're horrible people, but there is a balance here in trusting your loved one to feel able to come to you with any issues. Having a discussion with them beforehand where you express that you are a little bit nervous about saying the wrong thing, or a debrief after you've met any new partners to ask your polyamorous loved one how they feel about the meeting, can both help alleviate some anxiety you may have around meeting partners.

But in the end, this process can feel a little uncomfortable or awkward – and that is okay! Rather than judging yourself for your feelings, it might be wise to adopt a practice of seeing feelings as information that our brain is sending to us about the fears we have. We can be curious about those feelings and think about them without ruminating about them or seeing them as an inherent part of ourselves or a sign of something deeper.

You may be one of those loved ones who feel absolutely no nervousness around the thought of meeting your loved one's partners in the multiples, and if that is the case – brilliant! Some people don't have any anxiety about it and may just have a conversation with their loved ones about how they structure their relationships and at what point they might meet their partners.

As much as we don't always want to think about this, it may be worth having a conversation with your loved one about what would happen if they break up with any of their partners. Maybe you've already have this experience with your loved one regarding other breakups that they have had – but I do find that even though it is not uncommon for monogamous relationships to end and for loved ones to have built up some relationships with their loved ones' exes, rarely do people actually openly discuss any of this.

Think about your own personal relationships and what you might have wanted or do want from your family if and when you have gone through breakups. Obviously, how you might feel about continuing to associate with your loved one's exes in the future very much depends on the context of the breakup, but you never know what kind of relationships can build between people.

Speaking as someone who greatly values familial connections and has a significant lack of them in my life, I feel that if I had a partner and I got along well with their family, I may want to continue relationships there even if my partner and I ended our relationship, assuming the family wished to continue those relationships with me. If I were monogamous, it might be more cut and dried in terms of discontinuing relationships with people who may have become my 'in-laws' but with polyamory it can be a little bit more complicated.

Explore some of these scenarios with your loved one and see where their boundaries and expectations lie. It may be that the subject of meeting your loved one's partners isn't something you even need to explore or that some of these issues never really crop up, but showing your own initiative in understanding your loved one and their life by offering to meet partners and to be part of any journey they have in developing their relationships further is a very honest way of demonstrating that you are wanting to be there for them.

Personal Story: Sasha

Sasha was very committed to her religious beliefs in her youth and felt devastated coming into her agnosticism. Telling her parents about that felt like the first and most difficult 'coming out'. Soon after, coming out as queer was another unexpected development and admission, so by the time that she had told her parents about being polyamorous, there was less shock and reaction. As she had a limited dating history and no current partners at the time, her parents struggled to fully accept, understand or digest the implications and reality of what Sasha was sharing, especially as culturally, anyone who is not your spouse is likened to just being a 'friend'.

'It took a lot of re-explaining to get them to understand that I was in multiple, committed romantic relationships.' For Sasha, polyamory has been something she knew about herself for ever, even if it wasn't defined so clearly when she began dating. Even before she came out as pansexual and started to shift towards agnosticism, having an open marriage with an agreement and an understanding just made sense, and she had always wanted an open marriage. As she naturally came into dating and figuring things out, along with the increase of visibility of polyamory during the 2010s, everything seemed to shift into place.

Sasha practises a fair degree of openness with her dating life on social media, which has exposed some of her extended family to polyamory, even as her parents have taken a more hushed approach about her queerness, agnosticism and non-monogamy. Unfortunately this has led to some assumptions and harmful fallacies about what being polyamorous means which Sasha has had to combat. There have been moments where Sasha wishes her parents could have trusted her and approached her first instead of reacting with shock. She sees the approach her parents takes with many important aspects of her identity – her queerness, agnosticism and polyamory – as things that don't need to be discussed or talked about, which leaves Sasha feeling frustrated. 'People don't really recognize how cisheteronormativity is often very public and loud.'

Despite some of the obstacles, she is still close to her

mother and continues to have a bond with other members of her family. When Sasha had two partners she had both of them meet her family and had no issues with it, so there is light at the end of the tunnel. 'I hope that will continue to be how it plays out in practice.'

Personal Story: Rudy

Rudy grew up in a conflict-adverse family that felt a pressure to integrate and not cause a scene. Though more liberal-leaning, she remembers propriety being a big concern and the idea of 'What will the neighbours think?' always lingered in the back of her head.

While facing the pressure of completing grad school and feeling burnt out by trying to fulfil a partner's needs in a monogamous relationship, Rudy became more open to the idea of having multiple relationships, especially after having some close polyamorous friends who modelled loving, ethical connections. Eventually, her focus turned away from monogamy and more into polyamory and some connections stayed while others turned into friendships.

After feeling like there were so many joyful things in her life she couldn't share with a family she felt close to and not wanting to hide any more, she decided it was time to come out. While initially sceptical, Rudy's mom gladly read multiple articles that Rudy sent over as well as Janet Hardy's book *The Ethical Slut* and, after meeting Rudy's partners, became a polyamory advocate.

'My friends call me and will be like "Oh my god, your mom was at this dinner party and explaining the different structures you can have in polyamory and I learned a lot.'" Shifting away from feeling like she was hiding everything to feeling more open has made Rudy feel incredibly grateful, though she realizes that it's not always safe for people to be open with their families.

Some aspects of coming out have been less joyful. While her mother has been staunchly supportive, other family members requested a 'don't ask, don't tell' style of set-up and Rudy quickly noticed that they would be welcoming and normal around one partner, but awkward around discussions about another.

Rudy thinks some of this comes from the way polyamory sometimes forces others to look at their own marriages. 'If you take away the concept of marriage not being important and it doesn't look a certain way, you really start to examine your own marriage and say, "Oh, are we having a good time?"' Such a self-examination can be hard for people.

But Rudy couldn't help but feel judged and ashamed by the rule to hide her 'other' partner and finally she decided to set a boundary. 'It was empowering for me to just one day decide, you know what? This is me and I'm not going to try and make my life more palatable for you. Do you love me or not?'

Luckily, after expressing how wrong it felt for Rudy to hide parts of her life and after sitting on it for a couple of weeks, her family finally met Rudy's 'other' partner. 'I'm very grateful he was willing to be in a potentially emotionally charged situation in an effort to make my life and relationship with my family easier.' Once they finally met, Rudy's family realized that she was dating two really incredible people and became more open and accepting.

Despite some of the stereotypical questions and some

understandable fears that Rudy had been coerced into polyamory or might be in danger from the jealousy of men – which Rudy points out monogamy wouldn't save her from – the experience has been more positive than negative. 'I have never been okay with secrets. With honesty as one of my core values, I'm so glad everything turned out the way it did.'

5. TALKING WITH OTHER FRIENDS OR FAMILY MEMBERS

Find out immediately how 'out' your
loved one is or wants to be.
Discuss what would happen if somehow they were outed
to other family members and how you could help.
Really consider where your boundaries are with
telling your own parents or family members.
Offer the ability to help your loved one come out and to
provide the support and the defence they may need.

Not all polyamorous people feel the same way about being polyamorous, and we all have different comfort levels in terms of talking about polyamory with loved ones, extended family, work colleagues and more. Some of this can be very geographically dependent. There are definitely some places in the world where, depending on a variety of social factors, polyamory may be seen as especially deviant and may be grounds for a variety of legal action.

The sample size of polyamorous people may not be wide

enough for us to truly know on a global scale where it is 'safe' to be polyamorous in any and all contexts. While I don't know how common it is, I have heard of situations where individuals have lost custody of their children because their polyamorous status was seen as a sign of their instability. For this reason and many others, I think the safest thing for you to assume is that your polyamorous loved one's disclosure of polyamory is not currently something they wish to share with anyone but you.

It is far safer for you to be quiet about your loved one being polyamorous and to assume that it is not meant to be shared than it is to assume that because they told you, they are comfortable with more people than just you knowing. If you haven't already had a discussion with your loved one about who they are 'out' to and how much they want others to know, definitely have that discussion as soon as you can.

If you have already told someone you're not sure is 'safe' just yet, don't panic. As long as you let your polyamorous loved one know and promise to do better going forward, it is likely that the situation is addressable, if it's not something they need to be concerned about. It's important to know when you're having this discussion if there is any way you can facilitate their discussion of polyamory to wider circles and family members. They may not have a chart laid out of all of the people they definitely want to come out to just yet, but if you are a member of the family, there are definitely roles you can play that could be extremely useful.

I tend to find that in all cases of 'new' social phenomena that aren't actually very new, the assumption tends to be that the older generation can't 'handle' this information. Far be it from me to decide for you what your own relations can and can't handle, but I would encourage you, if your immediate gut reaction was that your older relatives aren't capable of wrapping their minds around polyamory, to challenge that assumption.

Before I even understood that my gender wasn't exactly normative, I distinctly remember a conversation I had with one of my relatives where they had offered me a present. The relative had remarked that the present might be a little bit too feminine for me. I wasn't and never have been very masculine-presenting, and have never been particularly sporty or had interests that would have put me in the 'tomboy' category, so I was pretty pleasantly surprised by how an older relative seemed to understand my gender better than I did at the time.

Older generations may seem very far away from us mentally, but they were young once and they often do have the capability to understand different social concepts and embrace them a lot better than younger people. People have such concerns about young children as well – and my response is very similar. Whether too young or too old, people assume that the only people capable of handling new and different social dynamics are people in the middle, and this is not necessarily the case.

Where you in particular can play a strong role, if you are a family member of a polyamorous person, is testing different topics on different family members to gauge their acceptance the concept of polyamory in a way that might help your polyamorous loved one make a decision about whether or not they want to come out to them. There are lots of different ways to broach a subject *similar* to polyamory that might help you figure out where another person stands. Because you are not polyamorous yourself, you may be able to broach these subjects with less fear and less consequence.

Depending on the family member in question and your own comfort levels, there are a few examples here of subjects you can introduce in passing to see what they think of concepts similar to polyamory:

- The 'hall pass': A lot of monogamous couples have a concept called the 'hall pass' which is a person, usually a celebrity, who they would be allowed to sleep with if they have the chance (usually with the understanding that this is unlikely to happen). This is a topic that could be easily more fun and jovial and which could help you gauge how someone feels overall about semi-open relationships.

- The celebrity couple: While celebrity culture may not be the best way to go about the subject of polyamory because it tends to be sensationalized and inapplicable to everyday people, introducing the subject that such and such couple is in an open or polyamorous relationship can give you an idea of what someone else thinks. Some notable examples are Will and Jada Pinkett Smith, Ezra Miller, Bella Thorne and Willow Smith (Wallace, Lavinia & Shearing, 2024). You could do a Google search on any recent stories on this as well.

- The Television Show: There are not many good depictions of polyamory in film and television and where there are examples, they are few and far between. The example that sticks out the most for me that isn't an immediately negative one was Catherine Zeta Jones' character Theo in *The Haunting* – but that is an older film by today's standards. Admittedly, romance films are not my favourite and this is not my forte so I would recommend doing some research yourself or visiting Genevieve of Chill Polyamory (www.

chillpolyamory.com/icouldnever) as she actively reviews film and television representations of polyamory. Bringing up one of these shows is a less celebrity-based way of introducing the topic.

Really, you can bring up the subject in any random way, but if you are concerned that it might seem that you are considering polyamory for yourself, the more timely the reference, the less likely this will be. When you introduce the subject, if someone reacts extremely negatively to the entire concept, they may not be the best person for your loved one to discuss polyamory with.

However, it's important to remember that there are people who are fine with the concept of polyamory so long as it's far, far away. Reacting nonchalantly or even positively to the subject in passing is no guarantee that they will react positively when told that a member of their family is polyamorous. Still, as someone who might be in a greater position of power to influence family members, you can perhaps do some of this footwork for your loved one.

Just be sure if you're going to do some of this work that you are happy with being able to deal with others' discomfort and that you don't mind so much if they start to believe that you want to open your own relationship and ask you questions about your *own* relationship. If you are in a location where it may be actively unsafe to be polyamorous, make sure you're aware of the risks of doing this work.

It's important that you don't go so far in terms of supporting your polyamorous loved one that you ignore your own boundaries and the state of happiness in your own life. This is a balance that your polyamorous loved one should be able to understand and respect. Make sure you're able to vocalize when you are uncomfortable with doing something or feel like being involved at a certain stage is inappropriate for you or beyond your comfort level.

I often advise polyamorous people to avoid becoming therapists for their partners and likewise would advise monogamous people to do the same. In this situation, I would also advise you to be willing to listen, be open and be kind, but understand that you're *also* not in an appropriate position to be a proper therapist for your loved one. Sometimes in all relationships people find themselves sacrificing their own well-being for that of others to such an extent that it becomes unsustainable.

In my experience, whether it involves monogamy, polyamory, friendships or any other type of relationship, whenever you betray yourself to satisfy other people and self-sacrifice constantly, the result is rarely if ever a closer relationship. Resentment easily begins to fester in environments like these. You can be a supportive loved one while also having boundaries and that is extremely important to remember.

Another aspect where you could definitely help when it comes to your polyamorous loved one being 'out' is by providing needed resources for them should they be 'outed' in a way they do not want to be. Whether that be work or within their family, you may be able to help them get legal counsel for anything they need to protect themselves against harassment, laws regarding adultery if they are married, or potential custody or other child-related disputes.

If you don't have the economic resources to help, being able to research some of these things ahead of time and find the resources they *could* contact should any of these problems arise can also be a clear way of providing your support and assistance. The critical aspect of this section is speaking to your polyamorous loved one about how 'out' they are now and to whom and how 'out' they would like to be going forward. Think to yourself what role you could play in their journey to discuss polyamory with wider family members or other social circles and how comfortable you feel being in that role. Honour what you're comfortable with and what you're not comfortable with and if you're in a place where practising polyamory is less safe or may cause them issues, see what support you can offer in terms of access to legal resources.

Personal Story: Adrienne

Adrienne grew up in a fairly liberal, left-wing household but still initially felt a little nervous coming out as queer to her family because, even though she lived in a household of retired academics who were pretty open-minded, in the area and culture in which she lived queerness was seen as something shameful and embarrassing. Though when a partner of hers transitioned, it did make the entire subject of queerness and polyamory a little easier to broach.

Polyamory wasn't something that Adrienne always knew about, and she stumbled upon the idea of different relationship types slowly. There wasn't a single moment where it clicked but rather a series of decisions, some good and some bad, including infidelity, that led towards dating someone who was polyamorous, but unfortunately they were an abusive partner who did a lot of damage to her self-esteem. After the rough breakup, Adrienne began rediscovering polyamory for herself, focusing on applying relationship anarchist principles (see the section '4. What Are Relationship Styles?' in Part 1) to all relationships in her life.

When Adrienne began dating a polyamorous person, despite the challenges of the relationship, she wanted to be open and honest to counteract her previous choices of keeping things a secret. This led to a series of predictable questions, sometimes honest and curious and other times feeling like mockery, more from siblings than from her parents. The largest struggle she found was the tendency for her family to use the network for communication, instead of directly telling others about polyamory.

This led to her disclosure of being polyamorous and asking family members to share the basics of her identity, but later having to correct the misinformation that she was a 'sister-wife' or fight off the idea that she was 'having an affair with a married man', which became emotionally exhausting. 'I wouldn't mind if they were saying things that were true, but the whisper network means information naturally gets twisted along the way, or people just misunderstand.' Adrienne also struggles at times to find emotional support for small polyamory disappointments, like meeting someone who is monogamous and having to tell them that she isn't single, or struggling with feelings rejection, where the response is often 'Well, you chose to live like this.' Setting boundaries has helped Adrienne ensure that there have been fewer hiccups over the years.

Despite some of the more frustrating challenges of feeling occasionally judged by siblings, such as them asking her to 'choose' between her partners and becoming angry when she asks them to 'choose' between their children, Adrienne doesn't regret telling her family about polyamory, but instead wishes that she hadn't had so many stumbling blocks on her journey to polyamory. 'I wish I had just known that monogamy wasn't the only option and had been able to live like that all along,' she said.

Personal Story: Wallace

Wallace grew up in a religious household with the expectation that they would be similar to their siblings – grow up and marry a nice girl who also shared the family's religion and settle down. For many reasons, this path wasn't something that Wallace felt was really suitable for them. Having both autism and ADHD created a lot of uncertainty in Wallace's life and caused a good deal of friction between them and their parents growing up. From those seeds grew a more complicated and difficult relationship.

They stumbled on polyamory after meeting someone at an event who said they had multiple partners and after going to a few events, eventually decided to try polyamory for themselves. There wasn't much in the way of reading books or even an inherent feeling of being polyamorous and it's something that Wallace is still exploring. As they began dating others and thinking of bringing partners to family events or even just answering their family's questions about their life, the thought of attempting to hide their polyamory from parents and siblings felt exhausting.

But discussing polyamory with their parents, just like their queer identity, wasn't something they completely wanted to embrace with both parents head on. Their queer identity hadn't necessarily dismissed, but it was more of a 'we don't want to know' – unless of course they were going to settle down as expected. While one parent tended to be accepting and kind about most things, the other parent tended to have a more strict and less compassionate approach to multiple aspects of Wallace's identity, including dressing in a more feminine way. 'Other people in my religious community accepted aspects of my identity, so I don't feel like being religious is the main barrier in my family for those who are more judgemental. Instead, I think it's more about neurodivergence or sometimes just downright ignorance.'

After a long-term relationship with a live-in partner ended, Wallace found a new relationship with a partner who was married with a husband. As the economy and their disability forced them to share a roof with their parents, the idea of hiding their private life became more exhausting. Wallace's siblings were a mix of judgemental and accepting, and that was a theme that carried into their parental relationships. While one parent seemed to embrace them overall, the other initially posed questions about whether or not their partner would 'leave them' for her husband. 'I explained to them that she is already "with" her husband, but they seemed to have a hard time wrapping their head around it.'

Despite the complications of their parental relationships, Wallace still attempts to have conversations about polyamory and other aspects of their identity and is often met with some interesting obstacles. 'When we were talking about how the usual path didn't really fit me and that I understood they just wanted me to settle down with a nice girl, their response was, "Why can't you be miserable like the rest of us?" which I honestly didn't know how to respond to.' Though partly this was said in jest, Wallace definitely struggles to feel hope that there will ever be some kind of breakthrough that will help their more judgemental parent understand. The story isn't necessarily finished when it comes to Wallace, their identity or how polyamory fits into their life, and they are still going through a process of figuring themselves out.

Conclusion

My hope is that throughout this book I've been able to provide you with some reassurance that your loved one is doing something that you don't need to worry about any more than you need to worry about them in monogamy. Polyamory is not inherently more free, safer, or anything better than monogamy. It's just a different way to do relationships. Polyamorous people are as diverse as monogamous people can be, so there are any number of ways that your loved one could be approaching polyamory.

While I've not been able to expand and cover all walks of life within this book, my hope is that I've given you enough of a background in polyamory in general so that you can understand a little bit more about it and address some of the main concerns that you may have had. After having read this, you might be in a better position to have discussions about polyamory with your loved one that will make them feel the acceptance and love that you undoubtedly have for them and bring your relationship closer.

If you've got this far in the book and you feel that you still don't fully 'get it', honestly I really don't think you should worry. You don't have to fully 'get' all aspects of your loved one to be there for them and support them. You don't have to be able to put yourself exactly in their shoes to respect them and their relationships. Sometimes I think there is an overemphasis on fully understanding everything about a certain concept in a way that may just not be easily accessible right away.

As your loved one goes through their life, just as much as they would in monogamy, there will be high and low points. The general concept of non-monogamy, as I have mentioned, is not necessarily new but your loved one is forging a path that they have likely not had any clear models for. Unlike monogamy, that brings with it a little bit of realistic trepidation and fear. You may not be able to advise them about this path, but you can be there to support them as they go down it.

It's okay if you don't get everything right. It's okay if you mess up. Even if you are a parent or guardian, you don't always have to be perfect, especially for your adult child. While I haven't had a child myself, I can say from experience of having these conversations and having them not turn out so well, that being a parent who is perfect is probably not possible. But being a parent who is willing to acknowledge their human faults and work forward with their adult child is what really matters.

Throughout this journey, I want to also emphasize how important it is for you to take care of yourself and remember that your boundaries and the things that you want to share about yourself, or not share, are also important. Being supportive doesn't mean sacrificing yourself. My hope is also that in learning to support your polyamorous loved one better, maybe this can also uncover ways to support yourself better in all of your relationships.

Give yourself the grace and understanding that you want others to have for your loved one and remember that you're also forging a path that likely hasn't been set for you by the society you grew up in. It's okay to be nervous, anxious, awkward and all of those things. Remember that you and your loved one are on the same team and I believe that, so long as you bring yourself back to that even in heated moments, you can resolve anything that comes up.

I hope this helps and good luck!

Lola Phoenix

Resources

If you've decided you want to do more than just provide support and want to understand a little bit more about polyamory and the different dynamics that might be involved, here's some further reading you can get stuck into to expand your knowledge even further.

BOOKS AND AUDIOBOOKS

Below I have included some of the basic books recommended to polyamorous people when they start out as well as some resources on complicated family dynamics, which might be something you encounter in your journey to support your polyamorous loved one.

More Than Two, Second Edition by Eve Rickert and Andrea Zanin: Specifically the second edition of this book is one that I recommend to people starting off in polyamory. It contains a lot of background information and understanding that can be useful for people starting out.

Rewriting the Rules by Meg-John Barker: I believe Meg-John has a really balanced and non-judgemental way of approaching a discussion of non-monogamy that is refreshingly different from some of the resources that a lot of people recommend.

The Smart Girl's Guide to Polyamory by Dedeker Wilson: One of the most common books recommended, which I feel comes from a less judgemental lens than a lot of beginner polyamory resources.

Love's Not Color Blind by Kevin Patterson: An under-recommended resource that delves into some of the aspects of being a person of colour within a polyamorous community that are often not addressed in other resources.

The Ethical Slut by Janet Hardy: While this isn't a book I could necessarily relate to too much as someone on the asexual (ace) spectrum, many people do recommend it because of how freeing it felt for them to read.

Opening Up by Tristen Taromino: Another book that is often recommended, which might be good to read out of curiosity to hear different stories about non-monogamy.

Polysecure by Jessica Fern: Though I am not personally fond of attachment theory, which underpins this book, a lot of people have found *Polysecure* super helpful in understanding their emotions and managing them.

Love Without Emergency by Clementine Morrigan: Clementine's work speaks to people who struggle with emotional ups and downs and surviving trauma while being polyamorous; I personally have found Clementine's work extremely helpful.

Sex at Dawn by Christopher Ryan and Cacilda Jethá: Though there have been many criticisms about this book, I appreciate the way it helped me challenge and reframe some of things I assumed were 'natural' and found it to be a really interesting read.

The Anxious Person's Guide to Non-Monogamy by Lola Phoenix: This is my own book, designed for people starting out or who experience a large amount of anxiety while practising polyamory. This may be something interesting to explore later on down the line.

How Does He Do That? by Lundy Bancroft: This book was pivotal in shaping my understanding of different behaviours in relationships and see them for what they can be. One of the things I love about it is that it's not about demonizing people but about understanding and identifying patterns.

PODCASTS

If you're more of an audio person and are interested in exploring podcasts about polyamory, here are a few I would suggest.

Multiamory: Covering a wide array of polyamory topics and having a variety of guests, the Multiamory podcast has a lot to offer to both polyamorous people and their loved ones, and I think it's a great way to get a bunch of different perspectives on different issues polyamorous people face.

www.multiamory.com/podcast

The Poly (Pod)Cast: A really lovely collection of different interviews building up on polyamory that explore different topics that might be interesting to listen to.

https://podcasts.apple.com/gb/podcast/the-poly-pod-cast/id1682693068

Chill Polyamory: One of my favourite resources for non-judgemental polyamory content that doesn't shame monogamy or any other types of relationship styles. Genevive's podcast features different interviews and experiences.

www.chillpolyamory.com/icouldnever

Non-Monogamy Help: My own podcast involves me giving advice to people who write in about their issues with non-monogamy and might be interesting in terms of exploring some of the common themes and issues that come up.

www.nonmonogamyhelp.com

THERAPEUTIC AND OTHER RESOURCES

Though not immediately polyamory related, I quite often find these creators have some really great insights into relationships that have helped me expand my own knowledge of relationships and communication.

Dan Savage: Dan gives relationship advice to a wide variety of people. I began listening to Savage Love before I even knew about non-monogamy, and as I have been even more sensitive in the past, I appreciate his approach to different topics on relationships.

https://savage.love

Todd Baratz: Todd's online content explores different facets of relationships and I appreciate that he challenges some of the prevailing narratives that people have about relationships in such a bold and straightforward way.

www.toddsbaratz.com

Africa Brooke: Africa has a lot of amazing things to say about self-sabotage that have really helped me challenge some of my fears and expand where I stand in different types of relationships. She has a great book and podcast that I find very intellectually engaging.

https://africabrooke.com

Hailey Magee: Though I wouldn't call myself a recovering people pleaser, Hailey's content has really spoken to me in terms of learning how to set and stand by my own personal boundaries and challenge the guilt that often comes with this in a way I find really accessible.

www.haileymagee.com

Rachel Wright: Rachel puts forth so much good, therapeutic content about relationships in general that challenges some normative perspectives in a way that's really understanding.

https://rachelwrightnyc.com

Whitney Goodman: Whitney has an amazing podcast and regular content on challenging relationships with family that I desperately wish I had access to years ago. If your family relationships are particularly challenging, I think that Whitney's content is helpful.

https://sitwithwhit.com

Matthias Barker: Though Matthias and I come from different walks of life, I love the way he makes me think about different concepts of trauma and how best to support people. He's got some truly great therapeutic perspectives that can be useful.

https://matthiasjbarker.com

Jessica Maguire: Learning more about my nervous system has been critical in learning how to manage my anxiety and how to combat it, and Jessica's content has been instrumental in that. If you want to learn more about how your fight or flight systems work, I can't recommend her enough.

www.jessicamaguire.com

Julie Menanno: Though, again, I'm not a big fan of attachment theory, I actually love the way Julie writes about it and makes the subject accessible. It has a lot more nuance than some of the attachment theory content I see out there.

www.thesecurerelationship.com

Alua Arthur: For me, a big part of appreciating my life is really facing the reality of my own mortality, which Alua Arthur and her content helps me do on the regular. There is something greatly healing about the way Alua approaches the topic of death as a death doula that I appreciate.

www.aluaarthur.com

Gabor Maté: One of the more famous people on this list, I love the way Gabor Maté talks about trauma and the way he challenges some of the perspectives of what we think about different disorders. I've always found his insights really helpful.

https://drgabormate.com

The Gottman Institute: Another well-known big name, The Gottman Institute puts out a lot of quality content about relationships that's always worth exploring and though I haven't seen them focus much on non-monogamy, I think they have a lot of great insights.

www.gottman.com

References

Anderson, J. (2014). The impact of family structure on the health of children: Effects of divorce. *Linacre Quarterly 81*(4), 378–387.

Asexual Visibility and Education Network. (n.d.). General FAQ. www.asexuality.org/?q=general.html

Borg-Laufs, M. (2013). Basic psychological needs in childhood and adolescence. *Journal of Education and Research 3*(1), 41–51.

Brock, R. L., & Kochanska, G. (2016). Interparental conflict, children's security with parents, and long-term risk of internalizing problems: A longitudinal study from ages 2 to 10. *Development and Psychopathology 28*(1), 45–54.

Bronson, F. (2024, February 7). Top 50 love songs of all time. Billboard. www.billboard.com/lists/top-love-songs-all-time/this-guys-in-love-with-you-herb-alpert-hot-100-peak-no-1-for-four-weeks-1968

Brown, A. (2021, November 19). Growing share of childless adults in US don't expect to ever have children. Pew Research Center. www.pewresearch.org/short-reads/2021/11/19/growing-share-of-childless-adults-in-u-s-dont-expect-to-ever-have-children

Carroll, C. (2021, June 29). Our unequal polygamous past. Institute for Family Studies. https://ifstudies.org/blog/our-unequal-polygamous-past

Caston, R. R. (2006). Love as illness: Poets and philosophers on romantic love. *Classical Journal 101*(3), 271–298.

Choi, H., Irwin, M. R., & Cho, H. J. (2015). Impact of social isolation on behavioral health in elderly: Systematic review. *World Journal of Psychiatry 5*(4), 432–438.

Dolan, E. W. (2023, December 1). New study confirms: Many adults opt for child-free life without regret. PsyPost. https://journals.plos.org/plosone/article?id=10.1371/journal.pone.0283301

Elwert, F., & Christakis, N. A. (2008). The effect of widowhood on mortality by the causes of death of both spouses. *American Journal of Public Health 98*(11), 2092–2098.

Grevenstein, D., Bluemke, M., Schweitzer, J., & Aguilar-Raab, C. (2019). Better family relationships–higher well-being: The connection between relationship quality and health-related resources. *Mental Health and Prevention 14*, 200160.

Gurrentz, B., & Mayol-Garcia, Y. (2021, April 22). Marriage, divorce, widowhood remain prevalent among older populations. United States Census Bureau. www.census.gov/library/stories/2021/04/love-and-loss-among-older-adults.html

Hughes, J. (2022, September 28). Whoopi Goldberg will not shut up, thank you very much. *New York Times Magazine*. www.nytimes.com/2022/09/28/magazine/whoopi-goldberg.html

Maté, G. (2010). *In the Realm of Hungry Ghosts: Close Encounters with Addiction*. North Atlantic Books.

McClellan, D. (2024, February 12). There's no biblical concept of sexuality or marriage [Video]. www.youtube.com/watch?v=0Mu4yYWj5-4

Meyer, T. (2021, February 11). Sweden and marriage. Sweden and Me: A Guide to Swedishness for Non-Swedes. https:// swedenandme.com/2021/02/11/sweden-and-marriage

National Alliance on Mental Illness. (n.d.). Family Members and Caregivers. www.nami.org/your-journey/ family-members-and-caregivers

National Scientific Council on the Developing Child. (2015). *Supportive Relationships and Active Skill-Building Strengthen the Foundations of Resilience: Working Paper No. 13*. Center on the Developing Child, Harvard University. https:// developingchild.harvard.edu/resources/supportive-rela-tionships-and-active-skill-building-strengthen-the-founda-tions-of-resilience

National Women's History Museum. (2017, February 13). The history of romance. www.womenshistory.org/articles/ history-romance

Nordgren, A. (2006) The short instructional manifesto for relationship anarchy. The Anarchist Library. https://thean-archistlibrary.org/library/andie-nordgren-the-short-instruc-tional-manifesto-for-relationship-anarchy

Rothblum, E. D., Krueger, E. A., Kittle, K. R., & Meyer, I. H. (2020). Asexual and non-asexual respondents from a US pop-ulation-based study of sexual minorities. *Archives of Sexual Behavior* 49(2), 757–767.

Ryan, C., & Jethá. C. (2010). *Sex at Dawn: the Prehistoric Origins of Modern Sexuality*. HarperCollins.

Saner, E. (2023, April 26). The rise of voluntary celibacy: 'Most of the sex I've had, I wish I hadn't bothered'. *The Guardian*. www.theguardian.com/lifeandstyle/2023/apr/26/the-rise-of-voluntary-celibacy-most-of-the-sex-ive-had-i-wish-i-hadnt-bothered

Sear, R. (2021). The male breadwinner nuclear family is not the 'traditional' human family, and promotion of this myth may have adverse health consequences. *Philosophical Transactions of the Royal Society B: Biological Sciences 376*(1827), 20200020.

Shah, V. (2022, July 25). The failures of American sex-education. Duke Center for Reproductive Health. https://dukecenterforglobalreproductivehealth.org/2022/07/25/the-failures-of-american-sex-education

Shearing, L. (2024, May 21). Why is celibacy so hot right now? *Cosmopolitan*. www.cosmopolitan.com/uk/love-sex/relationships/a60855327/why-is-celibacy-so-hot-right-now

Sheff, E. A. (2017, May 22). Child custody issues for polyamorous families. Psychology Today. www.psychologytoday.com/us/blog/the-polyamorists-next-door/201705/child-custody-issues-polyamorous-families

Thomas, L. (2010, December 31). The odd couple revealed: Helena Bonham Carter on why Tim Burton's snoring and her bossiness have driven them into twin homes. *Daily Mail*. www.dailymail.co.uk/femail/article-1342011/The-odd-couple-revealed-Helena-Bonham-Carter-Tim-Burtons-snoring-bossiness-driven-twin-homes.html

Thomas, P. A., Liu, H., & Umberson, D. (2017). Family relationships and well-being. *Innovation in Aging 1*(3), igx025.

Trevor Project, The. (2023, September 22). Acceptance from adults is associated with lower rates of suicide attempts among LGBTQ young people. www.thetrevorproject.org/research-briefs/acceptance-from-adults-is-associated-with-lower-rates-of-suicide-attempts-among-lgbtq-young-people-sep-2023

Wallace, M., Lavinia, E., & Shearing, L. (2024, March 5). 12 polyamorous celebrities who've opened up about

non-monogamy. *Cosmopolitan*. www.cosmopolitan.com/uk/
love-sex/relationships/g39137546/polyamorous-celebrities

Ware, B. (2011). *The Top Five Regrets of the Dying*. Hay House.

Washington, C., Gryn, T., Anderson, L., & Kreider, R. M. (2023,
June 13). Several generations under one roof. United States
Census Bureau. www.census.gov/library/stories/2023/06/
several-generations-under-one-roof.html

Yau, N. (n.d.). How much time we spend alone and with others. FlowingData. https://flowingdata.com/2022/05/12/
how-much-time-we-spend-alone-and-with-others